THE BULL
AND HIS HERDSMAN

ISBN 1 870609 02 6

CONTENTS

THE BULL
AND HIS HERDSMAN
A Zen Story from Ancient China

Commented on by
ZEN MASTER DAIZOKUTSU R. OTSU
From the German 'Der Ochs und Sein Hirte'
by Koichi Tsujimura and Hartmut Buchner

English translation by
Myokyo-ni

ZEN CENTRE
LONDON

TRANSLATOR'S FOREWORD AND INTRODUCTION

Around 1965, in my fifth year of training as a lay student at the Daitoku-ji monastery (Kyoto), somebody gave me a badly scorched copy of a book in German. It happened to be the only still readable copy rescued from a fire in one of the storerooms of Shokoku-ji monastery. I no longer remember who that veritable messenger of the Dharma was; but after another dusting, this little gem of a book emerged like a phoenix from the ashes!

The Dharma is the way all things really are, and at the realization of this way the ascetic Gautama became Buddha. However, this insight is not just intellectual, but is a live functioning. This Dharma, weaving coming-to-be and ceasing-to-be from causal connections and affinities, is self-propelling, self-evolving and self-voiding, yet is essentially without a self. Its grandiose neutrality is total and inspires awe as well as wonder; it is so great and all-embracing that with our finite minds we cannot help but read a 'meaning' into it — which does not exist as such, yet in a way exists.

Nowadays, among all kinds of books on 'Zen', the 'Ten Bull Pictures' have become specially popular, with diverse new drawings and commentaries. Common to them all is the lack of the 'deeply hidden subtleties' that Master Chi-yuan said he had discovered in Master Kuo-an's pictures — and so no doubt in his own heart as well. Those in genuine Zen training cannot but also discover these subtleties with the help of the traditional pictures of which Shubun's are supposed to be the perfect copy.

[For further details, see 'Epilogue']. Certainly they show the subtleties mentioned by Chi-yuan. To cite just one of the many in each picture, Picture I shows the seeker divided in himself, or 'estranged from himself' with feet pointing in one and the head in the opposite direction! These subtleties emerge in the course of training and are its hallmark. Shokoku-ji rightly treasures their possession of the pictures, and another 'meaningful' coincidence is that this commentary, genuine in content and style, comes from a past-master of Shokoku-ji as he addresses the monks training under him.

Considering the events during the years that elapsed since the scorched copy was handed to me, I cannot help but wonder whether there might not be a third, even more significant coincidence in the making. Master Otsu's commentary together with the actual text was translated from the original first German edition into English by Malcolm Trevor. Somehow his quite excellent translation ran into obstacle after obstacle 'as if' the Dharma itself was holding it back, not judging the time appropriate. I have long been aware of the need for just this book, which gives such concise and genuine pointers to Zen training and covers the complete process of transformation. Having myself in the course of training discovered some of the 'hidden subtleties', I have often used the pictures and text in showing students what training in Zen actually entails. Being urged to publish my own comments only increased the desirability of publishing Master Otsu's profound commentary.

Then suddenly another series of meaningful coincidences brought direct contact with Dr Buchner himself, from whom I learnt that the German original, far from being out of print, was in the second revised edition, and with the same publisher. Dr Buchner generously sent a copy of the revised edition and agreed to an English translation, which also was seconded by Professor Tsujimura. Suddenly everything seemed to come together and the book 'wanted' into print! Only I as the translator tarried for lack of time — and in the end even that seemed to have been to the advantage of the translation, for the rough draft was done within a period of three weeks which suddenly became free in the guise of a working retreat, when a combination of bad weather and bad 'flu' kept me, rather enthusiastically, at the desk!

Dr Buchner generously supported the project throughout, and apart from making available the new edition also supplied the information from Professor Tsujimura that the Japanese text had never been published and that neither the MS nor the tape still exist. Professor Tsujimura specially stressed that he was in touch with Dr Buchner all through the translation into German, and is confident that it truly renders Master Otsu's teaching. Although I myself have never heard Master Otsu's Teisho, twelve years training at Daitoku-ji under two masters has brought some familiarity with the Teisho style of Japanese Zen masters to their monks. Translating from the German, somehow from underneath or beyond, Master Otsu's sonorous Japanese sounded through, not infrequently supplying a term I was not familiar with in German but intimate with in Japanese! Thus the translation proved to be a joyous labour of love, carried out with respect and deep gratitude. Grateful acknowledgement is also made for felicitous phrases retained from the Trevor translation.

As to the translation of the Chinese text, I have translated the character denoting 'cattle' as 'bull', thus differing from the German 'Ochs' and the usual English translation of 'ox'. The ox is a patient beast of burden, strong and docile, in no need of 'long and painful training', nor is a cow; but a bull is. It is the bull that needs a nose-ring, not the ox! Correctly we speak of bull-fighting and not of ox-fighting. The latter is unheard of because the ox does not fight. The sheer strength and vitality, the magnificent splendour that is not without danger, together with the difficulty of taming and gentling, are all qualities of the bull, and illustrate the seeming impossibility of the task. So bull it has to be to get the connotations right in what is required for a training that involves nothing less than the taming and gentling of our own heart-bull. To begin with, 'stubborn self-will rages and wild animal nature rules', and again, 'bull' conveys the magnitude of the task ahead and also its 'greatness' in both connotations of the word.

Most English readers will be more familiar with the Japanese readings of the names of well known Chinese masters, and these have been added in square brackets, which latter also indicate translator's remarks.

Master Otsu's comments necessarily address the Zen student already in training under a master, and in remarkable detail expound the Koan training as used in the Rinzai Zen School in Japan ever since Master Hakuin (18th Century), the great renovator of this school. It is therefore taken for granted that the hearer/reader is familiar with the Buddhist background, basic as well as Mahayana, and with the general tenets of Zen Buddhism.

Much misinformation surrounds the term 'Koan'. Although perhaps over-simplified, the following analogy might help the reader who is not familiar with this practice. When asked what cold is, there is a moment of feeling cold all through and an involuntary shiver overcomes one; which, naturally, pre-supposes familiarity with 'cold'.

For the translation of the Chinese text, I have used the 'Record of Four Sections', a collection of four 'classics', one of them being the 'Ten Bull Pictures'. It contains the Chinese text, Japanese translation, and detailed notes. Since I used this book when hearing Teisho given on these four classics, my own Teisho notes taken at that time also proved useful and made this text an obvious choice. If some liberties were taken with the poems in an attempt to render the beauty of the symbolism into English, this has hopefully been balanced by great care in keeping faithfully to the meaning.

It is hoped that today when so many people are bewildered by the pace of life, with diverse remedies being advocated, this little book may point a way to a meaning that is straightforward and genuine. Master Otsu speaks with the quiet dignity of 'one who knows', and thus carries conviction. Such a one has no need to deploy fancy tricks, vulgarity, or to resort to imitation. Having 'produced' two illustrious heirs, he proved himself a true link in the living chain of the traditional transmission, and his experience at guiding others shines through the pages of this little book. May it also shine into the heart of the reader and bring an intimation of what genuine Zen training entails in time and effort, what it points at, and where it aims to lead those willing to undertake it.

Acknowledgments: First and foremost thanks go to Dr Hartmut Buchner for his support and generosity throughout, including his contacting the German publisher, Neske, who generously allowed special terms for the first English edition, and also secured agreement to and support for the English translation from Prof. Koichi Tsujimura.

Fred Zeserson typed the MS; thanks go to him and Kersti Haliste for proof-reading and helpful suggestions, and to John Swain for designing the cover and for the art work.

The photographs are reproduced from the German edition. Fred Zeserson also saw the MS through the press, in happy and helpful cooperation with Maggie Spooner.

Shobo-an, June 1989.   Myokyo-ni

The Chinese Text

INTRODUCTION BY MASTER OTSU

The one Great Matter we Zen Buddhists aim at may be expressed by 'A special transmission outside the scriptures — not depending on written words — directly pointing to the human heart — seeing into its nature and becoming Buddha'.[1] Thus exhorted we must not hold to any views, nor cling to any words whatever. Our one goal is to see into our own heart or original nature that is inherent in all human beings, and to have the Buddha-Dharma function free and unhindered, here and now.

As to the ten pictures, what actually does the bull stand for? From of old the activity of Samantabhadra was likened to an elephant just as the lion stands for the wisdom of Manjusri. By analogy, the bull indicates our own heart or original nature, what we call the original face, the Buddha-Nature, or the source of truth.

Bodhidharma introduced Zen Buddhism to China, but it was only after the Sixth Patriarch Hui-neng [Eno] that the school began to flourish. His line became known as the southern school, but there also existed a northern branch under Master Shen-hsiu [Jinshu]. The character of southern Zen is expressed as 'In the origin nothing exists. There is no place where dust can settle'. Or also, 'To jump in one leap directly into the place of the Buddha', which means to discover right here

[1] Attributed to Bodhidharma.

and now, immediately, the heart-ground and so to break into the origin of the Buddha. This sudden awakening is the basis of southern Zen. In contrast to it, northern Zen insists on gradual training in which the disciple practises step by step and finally becomes Buddha. Our Ten Bull Pictures show such a gradual approach and we may assume that they belong to the northern line.

Master Kuo-an [Kakuan] lived around 1150 at the Liang-shan temple in Ching-chou. He was a Dharma heir of Tai-sui Yuan-ching [Daisui Genjo] in the twelfth generation after Lin-ji I-hsuan [Rinzai Gigen], founder of the Rinzai line. Out of compassion for his disciples he drew Ten Bull Pictures [those illustrated are 15th century Japanese copies] and composed the first set of poems to go with the pictures.

These ten poems are in the Chi-chua style of four lines of seven characters each. Their subject is usually the beauty of birds, flowers, wind and moon, or of animals, birds, insects and fish, or again of mountains, rivers, grass and trees, or of the customs, habits, moods, and modalities of men. Master Kuo-an's poems differ from that; a Zen verse must contain the Zen truth or it is not a Zen poem.

Also transmitted with these ten pictures and poems is the Foreword by Master Chi-yuan who is of Kuo-an's lineage. In addition to the general Foreword, he also penned a short Preface to each of the ten pictures. Two later Zen Masters, Shi-gu Hsii and Huai-na Tai-lien also composed ten poems each to match the pictures. It is usual to reproduce them together. A later set of Japanese poems by Shotetsu of Tofuku-ji in Kyoto is here omitted.

We learn from the Foreword that Master Ching-chu [Seikyo] was the first to draw bull pictures. Though inspired by these, yet Master Kuo-an's bull differs from Ching-chu's which is all black in the beginning, and gradually changes from black to white.

Kuo-an's series starts with a herdsman looking for his heart-bull [his own heart and true nature]. This search leads him deep into the mountains. First he finds the traces, then he catches a glimpse of the hind-quarter. Eventually he succeeds in catching the bull, but needs to tame and gentle him, and finally he returns home riding on his back. Then he forgets his bull, and his own self. Where everything is cleanly forgotten, he suddenly plunges into the region of selflessness. At the last stage, 'Entering the Market-Place with Bliss-Bestowing Hands', the herdsman returns to the world, here, to take an active part in the life of the busy street amid the throng of people. By his living and in all his actions, his opened heart both proclaims and reveals the Buddha-Dharma.

Picture I then portrays the first aspiration as it has arisen in the heart of the herdsman-trainee. The next few pictures, up to VI, illustrate stages in the trainee's heart as he diligently practices and strengthens himself. The genuine and true balance in Zazen and Samadhi is not easy; to reach it, long forging and tempering are needed. During that period, thinking may be of use, but on the approach to Pictures VII and VIII, true religious experience is required. There the disciple must be completely detached and cut off from all words and speech, even from thinking. Only then can the change occur, the turning round and becoming one with one's own heart, with the true nature. Nobody can arrive there by mere thinking and theorizing.

Trainees intent on walking the Zen Way must have but one aim. This aim the Ten Bull Pictures illustrate clearly, and in the correct order, and so are an excellent guide. Yet however skilfully Zen might be expounded, no exposition will ever amount to being Zen itself which is ever and always a direct verification.

CHI-YUAN'S FOREWORD

This foreword to the Ten Bull Pictures was written by Chi-yuan. Master Kuo-an [Kakuan] lived in the Liang-shan temple in Ching-chu.

The real source of all the Buddhas is the original nature of sentient beings. Through delusion we fall into the Three Worlds, through awakening we suddenly leap free of the Four Modes of Being. Therefore there is something for the Buddhas to do and something for people to carry out. In compassion the old sage set up various ways to teach his disciples sometimes the complete and sometimes the partial truth, leading them suddenly or gradually from the shallow to the profound, from the coarse to the subtle. Finally one of his disciples responded with a smile. He was foremost in the practice of letting go, with eyes like blue lotus. Since then the treasure of the true Dharma Eye has spread everywhere, and has reached even our country.

One who has attained to the core of this truth soars without trace like a bird above all laws and norms. But one attached to the manifold things is caught in speech and misled by words; he is like the clever turtle that tried to wipe out its footprints with its tail — thus making them the more conspicuous.

Long ago, Master Ching-chu [Seikyo], aware of the different abilities of sentient beings, adjusted his teachings to the capacities of his disciples and prescribed remedies according to their respective illnesses. To this purpose he drew pictures of gentling a bull. First, with the bull becoming gradually white, the growing development of the disciple is shown; next the spotless purity of the bull shows the ripening of the trainee; finally, 'both man and bull vanished' illustrates the forgetting of both I and things [surrounding circumstances]. Though at this stage insight has already pierced through to the root, within the surrounding circumstances something remains that is not yet clear. At this point those of shallow root ability tend to fall into erroneous doubt, while others whose understanding is as yet only small or medium, become bewildered and wonder whether they have fallen into empty emptiness, or conversely whether they have been snared by the concept of eternalism.

I also saw another set of Bull-Pictures, by Kuo-an [Kakuan], with a poem to each picture. Like Master Ching-chu [Seikyo] before him, he put his whole heart into the execution of the drawings, and the ten poems shine into and reflect each other.

Kuo-an's Bull Pictures start with the bull being missed and continue until the 'Return to the Origin'. These pictures answer the requirements and diverse capabilities of trainees as accurately as food and drink appease hunger and thirst. With them to guide me, I, Chi-Yuan, have searched for the profound meaning and discovered deeply hidden subtleties, just as the jellyfish uses as eye the swarm of tiny shrimps that hide under it.

From 'Searching for the Bull' to 'Entering the Market Place', like attempting to draw a square circle, my prefaces try to describe the indescribable, thus needlessly disturbing the peace of men. There is no heart to look for, even less so a bull! How strange the one who here enters the market place! Unless the heart of the ancient masters has been matched in its very depth, the [resulting] wrong will spread to the successors. Truly my own Foreword has come from the depth of my heart.

COMMENTS BY MASTER OTSU

Buddha is the Awakened One. He is also called 'The Whole Heart'. The moment we awaken we are Buddha, awakened ones. This is not an invention of Sakyamuni but goes back to those before him. As far as Buddhism is concerned, however, he was the first to realize the Buddha-Nature. On the morning of the eighth of December, coming out of a state of deep absorption and looking up, he beheld the morning star and awakened. From this insight he exclaimed, 'How wondrous and wonderful, all sentient beings are fully endowed with Buddha's power and wisdom.' The content of this realization is 'self-evident verification'. Whatever is seen or heard in this 'self-evident verification' is all Buddha, and the source of all the Buddhas is the original nature inherent in all sentient beings.

The 'Three Worlds' are, respectively, the realms of desire, of form and of no-form. Together, these comprise the world of human beings. As long as we grasp at anything outside or inside, we are under the sway of delusion, and so caught in it. The Four Modes of Being are being born from the womb, from the egg, from moisture, and what chances to come into being by some change or transformation. This accounts for all animate and inanimate being. The same leap that carries directly into the realm of the Buddha suddenly delivers from the realms of animate and inanimate being. However, this must not be mistaken for a negation or denial, it is rather the great affirmation of everything, but free of all attachment.

Through delusion we sink into the Three Worlds, through awakening we suddenly leap free of the Four Modes of Being. So there is something for Buddhas to do and for people to carry out. Nothing like this exists in the realm of the real, but because delusion and awakening are now separate and distinct, both Buddhas and people have each to do their own tasks. For Buddhas it is, 'Sentient beings are numberless; I vow to assist them all'; and for people, 'The afflicting passions (Klesa) are innumerable; I vow to end them all.' To do so, since we habitually disport ourselves in the world of these afflicting passions, we need to return again to the home ground of the original nature. In this one way of ascending is encompassed the essence of Buddhism, and the foundation of a true and mature humanity. 'The old sage' is, of course, Sakyamuni, but by extension refers also to past Buddhas and masters. The 'compassion' is not contrived, not intentional, but rather wells up directly from the depth of the heart. Picture X of our series clearly shows this compassion. Compelled by it, Buddhas and masters say and teach what cannot be said or taught.

Tradition has it that the Buddha preached eighty-four thousand doctrines, and indeed, more than five thousand and forty volumes of scriptures have come down to us. The Dharma-Gates are manifold. Even in our Zen school there are seventeen hundred Koans or cases of Zen questions and answers. These manifold ways correspond to the differing abilities of trainees, excellent, middling or poor. Though in itself it is unnecessary to set up so many ways, yet compassion demands it. 'Complete truth' is the true nature of all that is, and this Sakyamuni taught to disciples with excellent ability. 'Partial truth' or one-sided truth then refers to the Hinayana teachings which in Mahayana Buddhism are considered to be provisional only, mere temporary means. Now, though some disciples may awaken on just hearing these teachings, yet others will be better helped by a more gradual approach which leads them 'from the shallow to the profound, from coarse to subtle'. The sum of the Buddha's teaching is condensed in this fourth sentence of the Foreword.

Wandering from place to place, the Buddha taught for forty-nine years. One day, a king offered him a lotus flower, and invited him to expound the Dharma. The Buddha assented, and before the huge audience he silently held up the flower. Nobody saw the meaning of this, and all remained as if deaf and dumb. All, that is, except his disciple, Kasyapa; on beholding the Buddha raising the flower, a smile spread over his face. The Buddha addressed him, 'In me is the true Dharma-Eye, Nirvana, the wondrous heart, true being and non-being. No words can ever reach there, and so it is transmitted outside the teachings. I now hand it over to you, oh Kasyapa.' This is called the 'transmission of what cannot be transmitted'. Since then the genuine Buddha-Dharma of the Zen school has spread from India to China and also to Japan. Pure and unchanged, this self-evident verification has been passed on through successive generations of masters as water that is poured from one glass to another remains itself clean and pure. The special transmission outside the teachings is of such nature.

Basic to the truth of the Dharma is the Buddha-Nature which is the original, inalienable nature inherent in all sentient and inanimate beings. The disciple trains to rediscover it. So when his master gives him a Koan he must work to become that Koan. When he has exhausted himself to the limit and has done one extra step beyond it, then the nature of this truth opens. This opening is called 'Satori' or 'Kensho', insight into the own original or true nature. At that, a spacious freedom opens which is not bound by any morals or reason, is outside just and unjust, good and bad, delusion and awakening, gain and loss, even beyond Buddha and Mara. Action is thus free and spontaneous in response, without any conscious intention. The only way to break into this state is by sitting meditation, and to that purpose the disciple must ceaselessly forge himself.

If a man is attached to things, then he gets caught by them and is led astray by words and talk. For example, he might have seen into his original nature and attained to the empty spaciousness that is free of all rules; but if he becomes attached to it, he is caught and confined by it. Even though awakened to the unknowability of absolute truth that is beyond understanding, this unknowing must not be clung to. And if not yet awakened, each word he says leaves a trace like that of the clever turtle and thus becomes an obstacle on the way towards trackless freedom and truth. Accordingly we must first break into a final depth and then return changed into the realm of sentient being. Mere belief in the true Dharma transmitted from Buddha to Kasyapa, even the constant recollection of it, is quite useless for we ourselves must experience that breakthrough. Apart from both Buddha and Mara, we must attain to the power of affirmation and say a great Yes to both Buddha and Mara, to the absolute and the relative truth respectively.

Jump suddenly and directly into the unconditioned and see into your true nature! This is exceedingly difficult. Master Ching-chu's [Seikyo] Bull Pictures (about 1050) point the way. His pictures show the bull black to begin with, and only gradually becoming white.

At first the bull rears and plunges between embarrassments and mistakes. But when the student diligently forges himself step by step in hard and bitter training, then from the depth of meditative absorption arises the strength to sit still and firm like a rock. Now the bull has become all white and is so powerful that with one breath he fills heaven and earth. This is called the ripening of the potential. Then the vanishing of both bull and man symbolizes the place of complete oblivion. There is nothing, neither bull nor man. Nothing, neither being awakened nor wanting to be awakened. When heart and world [I and things] have both been forgotten, a merger of both takes place. This is technically called the 'Treasure-Mirror-Samadhi' —

collected absorption in the mirroring of the heart-mirror. One mirror reflects itself in all mirrors, all mirrors reflect themselves in one mirror, and in each other. This mutually reciprocating reflecting is the reality of the real world.

In this utter emptiness disciples of shallow root ability or of medium to poor potential are apt to fall into difficulties and doubt, and for two reasons: one is that when they have broken into the nothingness that is void of both man and bull and there is neither good nor bad, they mistakenly consider it an empty nothing and consequently believe the real world to be just empty. This is called the 'view of nihilism'. Or they latch on to the opposite 'view of supposed eternalism' according to which the world lasts forever and man too continues after death. But a disciple of excellent ability does not get caught by either of these two erroneous opinions and will rather find differentiation in equality and equality in differentiation.

From the experience of his long and bitter training, Master Kuo-an put his whole heart into drawing his pictures and composing his poems. Hence they shine of themselves and in that shining reflect each other. In such play, heart and heart, Kuo-an [Kakuan] and his ancestor Ching-chu [Seikyo] mutually reflect each other. The great care with which Kuo-an has chosen each word is remarkable and deserves our respect and admiration.

Nothing is known of the priest Chi-yuan who wrote the Foreword to the series. As he says, he used Kuo-an's Bull Pictures as a guide in his own search for the wonderful truth of the Buddha-Dharma and in so doing uncovered 'deeply hidden subtleties'. These subtleties refer to the hidden, almost unnoticeable ways in which the Dharma acts and functions.

As to the jellyfish, little dwarf shrimps collect underneath and feed on its excretions. At the approach of a predator or any other danger, they quickly dive away into the depth and their sudden flight alerts the jellyfish.

In the primordial there is 'no heart to search for'. When Zen texts refer to 'no' and 'nothing' we need to be careful and always bear in mind that there is NO-THING. Even setting out to find the own heart and original nature of a human being, there is nothing to be found. We must learn there is that nothing to search for!

What magic! Something which actually is nothing is divided into ten stages and expounded in a spate of words! At the end of all this miracle-mongering even 'Entering the market with bliss-bestowing hands' has been conjured up! What silly nonsense — vanity of vanities! It is labour for nothing and again nothing!

I — SEARCHING FOR THE BULL

The search for what? The bull has never been missing. But without knowing it the herdsman estranged himself from himself and so the bull became lost in the dust. The home mountains recede ever further, and suddenly the herdsman finds himself on entangled paths. Lust for gain and fear of loss flare up like a conflagration, and views of right and wrong oppose each other like spears on a battlefield.

POEMS

1

Alone in a vast wilderness, the herdsman searches for his bull in the tall grass.

Wide flows the river, far range the mountains, and ever deeper into the wilderness goes the path.

Wherever he seeks, he can find no trace, no clue. Exhausted and in despair,

In the deepening dusk he hears only the cicada hum in the maples.

2

Looking only into the distance, the searching herdsman rushes along.

Does he know his feet are already deep in the swampy morass?

How often, in the fragrant grasses under the setting sun,

Has he hummed Hsin-feng [Shinpo], the Song of the Herdsman, in vain?

3

There are no traces in the origin. Where then to search?

Gone astray, he errs about in dense fog and tangled growth.

Though unwitting, grasping the nose of the bull, he already returns as a guest,

Yet under the trees by the edge of the water, how sad is his song.

Picture I

SEARCHING FOR THE BULL

Three qualities are said to be essential for walking the Zen Way, Great Faith, Great Doubt and Great Courage.

The disciple must aspire to the highest, and so needs to have great faith that this highest is attainable. Which means this great faith is not a mere belief but is already an active striving. Step by step the disciple gives himself into the training and works wholeheartedly on the Koan he has been given. Now great doubt has become essential as a spur to inquire ever deeper into the Koan question and into one's own questing self. Real Zen training consists of just courageous pressing on with the inquiry until the Koan is fully seen into.

Whatever mystic realm the trainee may break into, on no account must he settle there; rather from there he must do one more leap beyond. For example, he has been given the Koan of 'The Sound of the Single Hand'. Of course, *one* hand clapping does not make a sound! Yet the old sage insists it does. From that arises the question of what that sound could be — and also doubt about it. Without such doubt the question cannot lead to penetrating insight and awakening. Also, from constant questing and doubting accrues correct and joyous practice.

The third essential then is fierce courage — which means to

give oneself into the training with unshakeable determination and without any wavering. However much the disciple may believe or doubt, if he lacks this fierce, almost angry courage, he cannot fully complete his training. Only this fierce courage makes it possible for him to ignore all other interests and thus give himself exclusively into the quest. With burning determination he sets out to search for his true nature. At first he still lacks direction; the true nature, or Buddha-Nature, is inherent in us all, and so it is futile to look for it outside. Therefore, the determination to seek for it, this first aspiration, is in a way already the awakening — but in a way only.

TO CHI-YUAN'S PREFACE

The bull is inherent in his entirety and has never been missing. There is therefore no need to look for him. These first two sentences of the Preface point to the whereabouts of the bull, and also summarize the message of our picture series.

Coming back to oneself in an instant — that is awakening. Turning away from oneself is, accordingly, turning away from awakening. In such turning away a man gets lost in the things and circumstances of his surroundings and so becomes their plaything.

He is then unaware of the jewel in his own hand, searching the sky for the moon. If a disciple in this condition is given the Koan of Joshu's 'Mu' [Nothing], or the 'Sound of the Single Hand', then the 'Nothing' or 'Soundless Sound' pulls him this way and that way. Thus turned away, if he tries to grasp it conceptually, he falls into a kind of calculating intellectual juggling with the opposites, such as: if there is a Buddha then are also sentient beings; if delusion, then awakening also exists. Thus divided into worldly and holy, into delusion and awakening, the herdsman has turned away from himself and become estranged from the bull.

In the midst of equality the manifold distinctions arise due to delusion. In their interaction with the six sense objects (form, sound, smell, taste, touch, mental objects), the six sense faculties (eye, ear, nose, mouth, body, mind) give rise to thought. When the thoughts thus arisen are considered to be the true nature, afflicting passions and erroneous opinions proliferate and the own heart or original nature becomes lost in the 'dusts'. Utmost effort is required for seeking genuine truth, which entails listening to a wise master and learning to live in terms of that nature.

The home mountains recede ever further because the original nature has become lost in the 'dusts'. These mountains symbolize the home of the bull, of our original nature. Just when the herdsman is looking for the bull, by this very looking he has divided himself from the bull, and 'suddenly the herdsman finds himself on entangled paths'. Is he to turn right or left in his search for the bull? To the Sutras that contain Buddha's teachings? To the existentialists or the mystics? As long as he feeds on the left-overs of such learned meals, he will only stray about on entangled paths while inside him everything fights against everything, 'like spears opposing each other on the battle-field'.

TO POEM 1
(Kuo-an Shi-yuan) [Kakuan Shien]

The herdsman can see nothing but an endless wilderness all round. Looking at himself he sees only a worldly man lost in the wilderness of this world of delusion and error. With determined courage he has decided to let go of all other interests and to cut himself off from everything. Thus resolved he walks on step by step — through high grass, across rivers and mountains. This is the hard and bitter training, the forging and tempering. The river 'Desire' runs deep, and high soars 'Mount Stubborn'. In spite of his determination, the going is hard and the way of training continues endlessly. In the primordial there is nothing to search for — yet just there the herdsman must continue his search. Given the Koan of 'The Sound of the Single Hand', he must with all his might penetrate into the question of what this soundless sound of the one hand is, yet the slightest intention of seeking opens an unbridgeable gulf between the seeker and what is sought; so the river runs far and the mountains recede into the distance.

From morning till night the herdsman continues his search, through forest and jungle. He wants to find the truth and to equal Buddha and the old masters; but the flood of delusory passions and opinions, and the mountain of stubbornness prevent his sudden awakening to himself and becoming Buddha. Though he exerted his utmost effort, it was of no avail. Today, too, the sun has set in vain for the exhausted herdsman. In the deepening dusk only the hum of cicada in the maple trees.

TO POEM 2
(Shi-gu Hsi-I)

Hoping to find the truth in the words of others without oneself undergoing training is 'searching outside' without attending to one's own bull. In sages and masters this bull is no more complete than in us ordinary people.

The herdsman does not realize that his feet have already strayed into the swampy morass of afflicting passions and erroneous opinions. We need to look heedfully at the place where our own feet stand and not lose ourselves in some distant vistas. Wherever we go or stand, the bull is already right under our own feet and there is nowhere we can hide from him.

While the herdsman went looking here and there, the day has passed and the sun is setting. From primordial times to endless future, Buddhas and sentient beings are ever at home.

Though the herdsman has often returned home, he is not yet aware of it. 'The peasant uses it all day long but he does not know it.' The Sixth Patriarch Hui-neng said, 'The unborn, original source dwells amid afflicting passions and erroneous opinions.'

Hsin-feng is the name of a temple where Master Tung-shan Liang-chieh [Tozan Ryokai] once lived; thus it refers to the style or school of the herdsman's song. Not finding the bull, the herdsman kept singing this tune in vain. Yet it is in truth the wondrously beautiful melody from before the beginning of the world. Master Bai-chung, it is said, was struck deaf for three days when he heard this song. It is the same tune as the 'Sound of the Single Hand'. Everyone contains it, everyman sings it, but nobody knows it.

TO POEM 3
(Huai-na Tai-Lie)

All beings are endowed with the Buddha-Nature, hence all carry this bull within themselves. Neither awakening nor delusion are concerns of this bull; he is what each one has been from the beginning. Who then can search for him where? There is no need to search — yet, hidden in the question 'Who then can search for him where?' is the demand to set out and search; but how is it at all possible to catch the bull when 'in the primordial there is no trace'? Is it not impossible to find the bull at all? Well, yes, it is.

The herdsman has lost himself amid thorns and brambles, in the complicated world of speculating intellection. Entangled by his surroundings, he has forgotten the place where his feet stand. He seeks the bull that cannot be found, because his seeking self is itself the bull. In a way it might be said that the bull seeks the bull. We, the seekers, are also the sought; we and the bull are not two. So it is said of the herdsman that 'Unbeknown to himself, he already returns home with the bull.'

II — FINDING THE TRACES

Reading the Sutras and listening to the teachings, the herdsman had an inkling of their message and meaning. He has discovered the traces. Now he knows that however varied and manifold, yet all things are of the one gold, and that his own nature does not differ from that of any other. But he cannot yet distinguish between what is genuine and what fake, still less between the true and the false. He can thus not enter the gate, and only provisionally can it be said that he has found the traces.

POEMS

1

Under the trees by the water, the bull's traces run here and there.

Has the herdsman found the way through the high, scented grass?

However far the bull now may run, even up the far mountains,

With a nose reaching up to the sky, he can not hide himself any longer.

2

Many wrong paths cross where the dead tree stands by the rock.

Restlessly running round and round, in his stuffy nest of grass,

Does he know his own error? In his search, just when his feet follow the traces,

He has passed the bull by and has let him escape.

3

Many have searched for the bull but few ever saw him.

Up north in the mountains or down in the south, did he find his bull?

The One Way of light and dark along which all come and go;

Should the herdsman find himself on that Way he need not look further.

Picture II

FINDING THE TRACES

For a long time the herdsman has wandered about, through woods and along rivers, on high mountains and in deep gorges. Now he has found the traces. Where there are traces there must be the bull, the original nature of oneself. The disciple has read the Sutras and the records of the patriarchs, and has started Zen training under a wise master. He has now some general understanding of his own heart and true nature; but as this is still merely conceptual, he cannot yet be at one with it. Although he has some intimation of the undifferentiated nature, he still is helplessly lost in the world of differentiation.

TO THE PREFACE

Sutras are the collection of all that Sakyamuni taught after his awakening; the writings and collected sayings of the old masters make up the patriarchal records. Studying these, the disciple arrived at a conceptual understanding of the nature of the great Dharma, but however far conceptual understanding may go, it can never reach the nature itself. Only when the herdsman dares to take one more leap beyond this kind of knowing, as over the top of a tall tree, then he breaks into the region of truth.

From his study of the Sutras and records, he has also understood that the various utensils such as pots, kettles and knives, are all of the same metal, and that everything turns back into his, the herdsman's, own nature. The utensils stand for all the ten thousand things, and the one gold or metal for the own true nature. All that is, mountains, rivers, grass, trees, all sentient and inanimate beings, all are but the forms in which the own heart and original nature appear in response to circumstances. The deluded man is caught up in the variety of these differentiations and so cannot grasp how all are part of the one nature of truth.

Awakening, then, consists of taking in, at one glance, all that exists and directly understanding it as the nature of truth in response to circumstances. It has been said from of old, 'All being is but the one heart, and there is nothing apart from that heart.'

Up till now the herdsman has understood these laws of existence only intellectually, so he is not able to let the light of his own original nature shine; yet without this light his sight is not clear. Genuine insight is gained only by entrance into the realm of the real. Until he has transcended mere conceptual understanding, he cannot attain it, and so cannot distinguish true and false.

This realm of the real may be expressed as 'I look at the flower — the flower looks at me'. The herdsman cannot yet return to this his original home, and so it is said that only provisionally he has found the traces.

TO POEM 1

In the Sutras and in the records of the old masters the herdsman has found the traces of the heart-bull. But has he found the bull himself? All the afflicting passions and erroneous opinions stand up and obstruct the Way like an impenetrable thicket. And yet, the nature of truth is never hidden.

When he begins to train with the Koan he is given, the disciple, just like the herdsman, stands amid the afflicting passions and erroneous opinions. Should he think that he can simply throw these off and thus, free from them, may now look for his heart and original nature, he will never find the heart-bull. That meeting is possible only when passions and opinions are fully penetrated so that their very nature is seen into and can be experienced as truth, as true nature. The grassy jungle, the towering mountains, and the wide river are themselves the landscape of the heart-bull who cannot hide himself, for his nose encompasses heaven and earth. In all our actions — eating, undressing, lifting a hand, walking — the heart-bull is present. There are not two — a seeking self and a bull to be sought. The Japanese Zen Master Ikkyu once said, 'What is the heart? Though invisible, it encompasses heaven and earth.'

TO POEM 2

On the search for the original nature many illusory ways are encountered such as Protestant or Catholic in Christianity, or Zen, 'Pure Land', Tendai, Shingon, and others in Buddhism.

As if into a wild jungle, the herdsman steps into the vulgar knowledge and afflicting passions of the world only to become engulfed by them. If but one wave arises, thousands follow — and just so it is with deluded thoughts. Has he found the bull hiding in the tall grass and bushes? Is he aware that it is he himself who is hidden in the little cave of I and in it walks blindly round and round?

Training now in a Zen monastery, the disciple has found the traces of his heart-bull. At that, he breaks into a region where there is neither good nor bad, no delusion and no awakening. If this leads him now to the view of nihilism, he is still on a wrong path; if the understanding he has gained from hearing, seeing and reading prompts him to the view of eternalism, that is another wrong path. Yet he must catch his heart-bull amid just such wrong and entangled paths, amid worldly passions and deluded views. How can he do so?

Just when the herdsman believes that he has caught the bull, has understood the nature of truth, just then the attempt has failed; the bull has passed him by and escaped. The Sutras and the records of the old masters are not the bull himself, only his traces. Though these may lead to an understanding of the truth, such understanding remains purely conceptual. What comes in from outside is trace only. What Sakyamuni taught and what Bodhidharma said is not the heart-bull himself! Only by letting go of all of this can we meet the true heart-bull; and only then do we realize that our own heart and original nature is always and everywhere unchangeably present. This realization is then genuinely our own and is beyond all comparison.

TO POEM 3

The herdsman does not see the bull with his two eyes; rather by awakening he attains insight into the true nature of the looking self. No words can reach there. Within the limits of their consciousness and understanding, many seek the bull by following the words of the old masters, of Sakyamuni and Bodhidharma; very few, however, have transcended these limits and have seen into the heart-bull.

The herdsman was fortunate enough to find the traces — but where is the bull himself? Up north in the mountains or down in the south? Everywhere, mountains piled upon mountains; the way of the herdsman is hard. This bull is neither north nor south; he fills the whole world of truth! Has the herdsman found him? Does he not see him? Look at the place under your own feet!

'Light and dark' stand, first, for the world of opposites — delusion and awakening, gain and loss, right and wrong, good and bad, passion and wisdom, differentiation and equality. When the herdsman has found the one way of light and dark, it has already become his own nature and he is no longer in need of anything. Having turned round from outside to inside, when he now reflects himself from within, the heart-bull is present. Though he has already entered the one way of light and dark, he still holds on to awakening and sticks to delusion; thus ensnarled by words he lets the heart-bull pass by and escape.

The one way of light and dark is also the time of 'the pairing of light and dark'. At that time, light and dark, delusion and awakening, worldly passions and wisdom no longer oppose each other but pair and merge into one whole. That is what is called the 'Middle Way', the free way along which everything including the herdsman comes and goes, free and unhindered. Arriving at this place of 'the pairing of light and dark', the heart-bull is present.

III — FINDING THE BULL

The herdsman recoils startled at hearing the voice and that instant sees into the origin. The six senses are quieted in peaceful harmony with the origin. Revealed, the bull in his entirety now pervades all activities of the herdsman, inherently present as is salt in sea water, or glue in paint. When the herdsman opens his eyes wide and looks, he sees nothing but himself.

POEMS

1

Suddenly a bush warbler trills high in the tree top.

The sun shines warm, and in the light breeze the willows on the
water's edge show their new green.

There is no longer a place where the bull can hide himself;

No painter can capture that magnificent head with its soaring
horns!

2

On seeing the bull and hearing his bellow,

Tai-sung, the painter, surpassed his craft.

Accurately he pictured the heart-bull from head to tail,

And yet, on carefully looking, he is not yet quite complete.

3

Having pushed his face right against the bull's nose,

He no longer needs to follow the bellowing. This bull is neither
white nor blue.

Quietly nodding, the herdsman smiles to himself.

Such landscape cannot be caught in a picture!

Picture III

FINDING THE BULL

At the stage of Picture II, the disciple has realized the nature of all that is and has intellectually understood that all leads back to the one nature of himself. Now at the third stage he penetrates still deeper into the true origin of all that is and so comes to the Great Way which unites knowledge and action. At this stage, what the disciple says and what he does no longer oppose each other, and training and verification become one. All that is leads back not just conceptually but actually to his own original nature.

In the third volume of the Zen text Hui-yuan [Goto Egen] is the following story about Master Pan-shan [Pochi]. 'One day the monk Pan-shan went into the town. At the butcher's he heard a man ordering, "One pound of good boar meat, please." The butcher threw down his knife, crossed his arms and replied, "I only sell good meat, not one piece of bad!" On hearing this, the monk Pan-shan awakened.'

From this story we learn that everything, gain and loss, right and wrong, good and bad, genuine and fake, returns to the one nature of undifferentiated equality. The moment a wilfully

choosing will arises, or an opinion that is prompted by love and/
or hate, the heart-bull has already escaped. Without such wilful
intention, a man can let all that is become himself and so what is
can no longer turn him. The instant the man looks at the flower,
the flower looks at the man. In this region of the heart the
difference between 'mine' and 'other' has gone and the original
nature or 'True Face' is present. This is the time when 'the great
sky vanishes and the iron mountain shatters'. In this at-one-
ment of heart and surroundings the heart-bull shines through
all that the disciple does or does not do. But though the trainee
has entered this region of truth in the third stage, this does not
yet mean he has irreversibly become one with it.

TO THE PREFACE

An old saying is, 'On hearing sound to find the way; on
seeing form to see into the heart.' The place 'where the great sky
vanishes and the iron mountain shatters' is the heart-bull
himself. This quotation is from the Ryogon Sutra [Surangama
Sutra], the chapter on Kannon or Kanzeon [Avalokitesvara].
Kannon ('Seeing Sound') is the Bodhisattva who sees the sound
of all the world and the voices of all that is, and delivers all. One
strike of the bell, if we truly hear it, contains all the manifold
teachings. In such hearing we leap into the region where heaven
and earth meet on the tip of a finger. When on hearing the stroke
of the bell we instantly become one with it, our original nature is
present. Though the Preface refers to hearing only, it is not the
only entrance into the origin — it may be by seeing, hearing,
tasting, smelling, touching or thinking. If it penetrates to the
origin, each can bring to deliverance.

Hence, if the herdsman breaks into the origin by seeing,
deliverance simultaneously extends to all the other senses
because they are in accord with the bull and also with each
other. Inherently present as salt is in sea water, or as glue is in

paint, the Buddha-Nature in its entirety is present in all our doing. The seeing herdsman and the bull seen are at one and the same time both two and not two. When the herdsman now with wide open heart-eye looks into the nature of anything that exists, each and everything shines as the nature of the looking self, that is of the heart-bull.

TO POEM 1

It is a mild day in spring. This landscape of spring is the realm of the heart without dark clouds because the whole sky has vanished and the iron mountain is shattered. In it the disciple is beyond both understanding and delusion. Having become one with the Koan, there is no longer a self that works on the Koan — and yet there is a self.

From the most distant past into the farthest future, the heart-bull is present in mountains and rivers, in trees and grass, in all and everything. Once the disciple has seen him, there is nowhere the bull can hide from him, or he from the bull. The soaring magnificent horns express the mood of 'Reddish fog and blue-grey mist enshroud the world; scent of grass and flowers blooming in the fields — all is one spring'.

TO POEM 2

If the herdsman has found the heart-bull and has seen into his original nature, the murmuring of the valley brook is the voice of the Dharma, and the green mountain is the body of purity. As did Tsai-sung, who became famous for his bull paintings, so the trainee attained to the truth on seeing the bull and hearing his bellow.

The bull in Tsai-sung's paintings is said to resemble the heart-bull from head to tail; this means that detached from body and mind the disciple has himself become the heart-bull.

Heaven and earth are at one in this heart-bull, and not even a painter like Tsai-sung can fully portray him. The herdsman has broken into the wonderful realm of the heart which defies pictures and words; however great the artist, neither painting nor language can reach there; rather, it is from this realm that we paint and speak. Here is the place of the really ordinary!

TO POEM 3

After long and painful training the disciple's face collided with the nose of the bull. Now they are tied to each other and there is no more doubt and hesitation. The disciple no longer needs to search for words and meanings in the Sutras and records of the old masters, nor in the countless scholarly texts and treatises. He has discovered the bull in himself. When he now works on a Koan with fierce determination and penetrates into it, he becomes wholly one with it. The instant the herdsman meets the bull, the actual instant of meeting him, is neither white nor blue — it is outside the world of colour and form, beyond all differentiation. The old masters coined various names for this bull, such as 'mud-bull', 'buffalo', 'iron bull', but all names are provisional only.

The herdsman nods to himself, 'Now I see'. Pure joy wells up in him and a smile plays over his face. Neither self nor things exist here, and the herdsman feels as if he had swallowed all the seventeen hundred Koans at one gulp. 'Be happy in yourself! No other can give it to you!' Not even a master can hand it to his disciple. Hence the smile on Kasyapa's face when Sakyamuni lifted the flower. This landscape is beyond words.

IV — CATCHING THE BULL

For the first time today he encountered the bull that for so long had been hiding in the wilderness. But this pleasantly familiar wilderness still attracts the bull strongly. He yearns for the sweet-smelling grass and is difficult to hold. Stubborn self-will rages in him and wild animal-nature rules him. If the herdsman wants to make the bull really gentle, he must discipline him with the whip.

POEMS

1

With great effort the herdsman succeeded in catching the bull.

But stubborn, wilful and strong, this bull is not easily gentled!

At times he breaks out and climbs up to the high plains

Or rushes down into foggy marshlands to hide himself there.

2

Hold the rein tight and do not let go.

Many of the subtlest faults are not yet up-rooted.

No matter how gently the herdsman pulls at the nose-rope,

The bull may still rear and try to bolt back to the wild.

3

Though caught where the sweet-scented grass reaches sky-high,

The herdsman must not let go of the rein tied to the bull's nose.

Though the way home beckons clearly already,

The herdsman must often halt with the bull, by the blue stream
or on the green mountain.

Picture IV
CATCHING THE BULL

The herdsman comes to full insight into the heart-nature at the fourth stage of 'Catching the Bull', but this insight has yet to be verified and proved. 'Opening his hand and plummeting down the cliff, and after the last breath, surprisingly, coming back to life again.' The disciple has caught the bull, and this catching then becomes the region of the herdsman's own heart where he has insight into the Buddha-Nature and attains to the infinity of the Great Life.

TO THE PREFACE

Though the herdsman has seen into his original nature, he can not yet, or not always, 'let the right thought prevail'. For too long he has lived in the jungle of erroneous opinions and amid the dust of intellection. His bull is still wild, animal nature still rules him; he wants to drag the man back into the familiar world of the ten thousand things. The herdsman is still pleased when others praise and admire him, but when told off or slandered, he becomes angry or resentful. Thus his heart is still under the sway of praise and blame and is disturbed by them. Although he has caught the bull, he has not yet become his real life. Seeing the moon, he rushes after the moon; seeing a flower, he grabs at it. He does not yet know real freedom, cannot know it.

While the bull is still wild, nothing can be done with him. The herdsman must tame and gentle him, and strict discipline with whip and rein are essential. Even though the disciple has seen into his original nature, he must not stop there. An old saying states, 'The further one goes into it, the deeper it becomes.' To attain real gentleness demands, first, to return to one's original nature, and then to learn to let it function in all circumstances.

TO POEM 1

The herdsman has caught the bull. This, for example, may mean that in deep meditation on the Koan the disciple has suddenly penetrated to the very ground of his being. But even though he has died the 'Great Death' once, he is not yet beyond the danger of being swayed by still powerful erroneous opinions and passionate desires. Though in the monastery he has attained to a clear insight in his everyday life, he finds it hard to keep apart from all attachments. Frequently he still wants to turn off into a side-road.

The 'high plains' are free of dark clouds. In that region there is no Buddha above and are no sentient beings below, no afflicting passions and no wisdom. The disciple now stands at this height where there is no dust nor anything. The 'deep places of mist and cloud' then refer to the dark regions of the afflicting worldly passions. Although now attained to the place where there is 'no roof above, no ground beneath', yet not realizing it, the disciple is still lost in the dark region.

TO POEM 2

Determined not to let the bull escape, the herdsman penetrates ever deeper into the region of neither worldly passions nor wisdom. Slowly and carefully he keeps reining in the bull who ever again wants to escape to his old haunts. Training is now of utmost importance. The disciple must ceaselessly work on himself to 'always let the right thought prevail'.

TO POEM 3

Where the sweet-scented grass stands sky-high, at the boundary where delusory opinions and afflicting passions touch on wisdom, the herdsman has caught the bull. In the very midst of these opinions and passions he has awakened to his original self. Take care now, the bull is not yet gentle!

The disciple must not stop after the break-through but rather must again and again check himself in the mirror of the sayings of the old masters. Thus he continues the 'training after the break-through'. Having caught the bull, the herdsman wants at once to set out for home; the way there is already quite clear to him. However because the bull is not yet tame and gentle, he must often stop with him, now by the blue water, now on the green mountain. This is the painstaking training of 'always letting the right thought prevail'. Worldly passions still flare-up after the break-through.

V — GENTLING THE BULL

If but one thought arises, then another and another follows in an endless round. Through awakening, everything becomes truth; through delusion, it becomes error. Things do not come into being depending on circumstances but arise from the herdsman's own heart. Hold the rein tight and do not allow any wavering.

POEMS

1

Not for a moment may the herdsman drop whip and rein

Or the bull would break free and stampede into the dust.

But once patiently trained and made truly gentle,

He follows the herdsman without halter or chain.

2

Now the bull may saunter through the hill forests,

Or else walk the much travelled roads, covered in dust.

Never will he touch fodder from another man's meadow.

Coming or going requires no effort — the bull quietly carries
the man.

3

In patient training the bull got used to the herdsman and is truly
gentle.

Should he walk right into dust, he now no longer gets dirty.

Long and patient gentling! In one sudden plunge the herdsman
has won his whole fortune.

Under the trees, others encounter his mighty laugh.

Picture V

GENTLING THE BULL

At the previous stage, the herdsman has really caught the bull, but because of the very nature of this catching, he may become attached to him and in order to detach himself again, he must gentle the bull. Hence the necessity for the 'training after the break-through'! This consists of merging together both bull and oneself, so that the unity persists in all one's doing and not doing, in all situations and under all circumstances. At the same time this gentling also effects a fusion of oneself and one's surroundings. In this pure at-one-ment, self absorbs itself into the given situation and the given situation absorbs into oneself. The old masters tell us that it is difficult indeed to let this unity always prevail. The break-through is necessarily abrupt and sudden; but afterwards, until what has been attained can always prevail, much time is needed and training is gradual.

TO THE PREFACE

In itself, the break-through to awakening is at the same time a looking back at the nature of ordinariness. In this hindsight, the endless streams of thoughts, formed and activated by the afflicting passions, are directly and immediately transformed into wisdom. Deluded, the disciple is under the sway of erroneous opinions and calculating intellection, and so is driven by the coming and going of all things. Through awakening, the endless series of thought following thought becomes the world of truth, the one world of Nirvana. Through delusion it becomes the world of suffering, Samsara, the world of birth and death (neither of which exist in the primordial). This is seeing it from the point of view of the 'relative truth'.

How it looks in the light of the 'absolute truth' is expressed in the Zen saying, 'Everything one strip of iron. Mountains and rivers, heaven and earth, all pitch-black'. Here, there is no Buddha above and no sentient beings below, the willows are not green, the flowers are not red; there is no awakening and no non-awakening, no delusion and no non-delusion, no afflicting passions and no wisdom, but one must not stop even here. There are no beings without [inherent] nature and no [inherent] nature without beings. Without the world of the absolute there is no realm of the paired opposites [the world of the ten thousand things]. Without equality there is no differentiation, without differentiation no equality. Therefore it is said in the Heart Sutra, 'Form is emptiness, emptiness is form.'

While we can see only things, or only our original nature, we cannot enter the world of truth. Awakening 'opens' only when things and our original nature have fully merged into one, that is when we have returned to the region where all is one, to the unifying recollection which is the moment of the 'Great Death'. When the disciple now sees into a Koan, there is neither the Koan nor the seeing self, and yet both are there, the one and the other. Koan and self have become one above all negation and affirmation. Once the disciple has arrived there he is no longer driven about by anything. The world of the ten thousand things arises from his own original nature.

TO POEM 1

'Whip and rein' refer in particular to the Koans the disciple has been given, and also to the teachings and sayings of the old masters. If he wants to make the bull really gentle, the disciple must hold on to the Koan whatever he may be doing, keep looking into the Koan and collect himself in the training. A sudden break-through is relatively easy, but training after the break-through is hard indeed. Besides, there is always the danger that the disciple may relapse and fall back into the old habits, into his old world.

Once the herdsman has gentled the bull after long and hard training, the bull follows him like a shadow. Now the disciple can let his own self and the surroundings always be one, that is, 'let the right thought prevail', everywhere and always. In joy and in sorrow, angry or laughing he is at one with his heart-bull. But not until he surpasses Buddhas and patriarchs must he cease from his efforts.

TO POEM 2

The disciple has now arrived at the mountain top, the place where there is no wisdom to seek and no 'birth and death' to escape from. This utter detachment is a desert without grass, the realm of equality [non-differentiation], the home of the original nature. On that mountain the bull finds plenty to eat and drink so that he can have a good day there. However the disciple must not stay in this region of equality, but must go down into the dust of busy roads, into the crowded market-place. There he must shoulder heavy burdens and pull the loaded cart, begrimed with the dust of horses. He immerses himself in the world of differentiation to assist sentient beings lost in it.

The first and second lines also express the determination to seek wisdom and assist sentient beings. The true bull must himself be both, ascent and descent. 'When he enters the ordinary world he does nothing wrong or bad' refers to the morality and the laws of the ordinary world.

What a Zen trainee aims for is contained in the vow, 'Sentient beings are numberless, I vow to assist them all'; but in so doing he must never harm anything. No action engendered by the heart-bull can be outside the borders of morality and law. Rather, such action is in itself the source of all morality and law.

The statement 'The bull quietly carries the man' does not really match this fifth stage, for the herdsman cannot yet bestride the bull. One wonders how such a mistake could arise; one opinion has it that the picture Shi-gu [Hsi-I] had before him when he wrote this poem did indeed show the herdsman sitting on the bull. This is unlikely, however, for then surely more than one divergence would have arisen in the series. For whatever reason, it does not correspond to Kuo-an's picture.

TO POEM 3

The herdsman has wholly become one with the bull. When he now returns to the dust of the world, he no longer gets dirty. The fish in the ocean is not salty itself; water birds themselves are not watery! There is an old Zen saying, 'To one absorbed in Zazen, the heavy traffic on a crowded road is just like seeing the trees in a mountain forest'.

The disciple acquires his strength when he falls down in the training. The moment he stumbles and crashes down he forgets the bull and himself. At this moment of forgetting, the willow loses its green and the flower its red and even this losing voids itself. Only when the disciple has passed through this crashing down and losing himself, can he attain to a real and great awakening; only then does the break-through become genuine.

At the moment of crashing down, 'birth and death' vanish of

themselves and so does Nirvana. It is just in this voiding that both, 'birth and death' and Nirvana, are truly themselves. A man who has reached there is beyond praise and blame, and even Buddhas and patriarchs cannot find him, but his mighty laugh can be heard everywhere. It is said that Master Yueh-shan [Yakusan] one night walked up a mountain track and on seeing the moon broke into such a great laugh that it was heard twenty miles away.

'Gentling the Bull', the time of steady, constant training, is also called 'the long and patient maturation of the holy womb'. One of the greatest of the Japanese masters, the National Teacher Daito, spent twenty years after his break-through under a bridge among beggars. His Dharma heir, Master Kanzan, worked as a hired labourer in a mountain village. All the old Chinese masters also matured themselves in such training.

VI — RETURNING HOME
ON THE BACK OF THE BULL

Now the struggle is over! Gain and loss, too, have fallen away. The herdsman sings an old folk song or plays a nursery tune on his flute. Looking up into the blue sky, he rides along on the back of the bull. If someone calls after him, he does not look back; nor will he stop if tugged by the sleeve.

POEMS

1

Without haste or hurry, the herdsman rides home on the back of
   the bull.

Far through the evening mist reaches the sound of his flute.

Note for note, tune for tune, all convey his boundless mood;

Hearing it, no need to ask how the herdsman feels.

2

Pointing ahead towards the dyke where his home is,

He appears out of mist and fog, playing his flute.

Then suddenly the tune changes to the song of return.

Not even Bai-ya's masterpieces can compare with this song.

3

In bamboo hat and straw coat he rides home through the
   evening mist,

Sitting back to front on the bull, joy in his heart.

Step by step the bull walks along in the cool, gentle breeze,

And no longer looks at the once irresistible grass.

Picture VI

RETURNING HOME ON THE BACK OF THE BULL

The man is now free of himself, and the bull too is free of himself. The man, thus free, leisurely playing his flute, rides along on the bull; and the bull, also free of himself, walks along quietly. Playing the melody of the unborn, man and bull are on the way home. Where heart-bull, herdsman and world surroundings are returned to and recollected in the one nature, the herdsman absorbs into the bull and the bull into the herdsman. The donkey sees the well and the well sees the donkey. The bird looks at the flower and the flower looks at the bird. This is called 'The Recollection in Awakening.'

The one nature is in all things and all things reflect the one nature. Here prevails the oneness of man and bull; self and others being the same, this is the union of man and world. An old Zen master calls this region 'snow piled on a silver salver', or 'a white heron hidden in the light of the full moon'. Here everything is of the One Nature. Mountains and rivers, heaven and earth, moon and stars, all are the true face of the patriarch. In the great letting-go-of-everything there is no injustice and no loss, neither dust nor delusion. Here everything is clean, fresh and open. This is the time of the truly 'great leisure'.

Volume four of the Zen text Hui-yuan [Goto Egen], the chapter on Master Chang-ching Ta-an, has a story that illustrates the 'Return on the Back of the Bull'. The monk Ta-an once asked Master Bai-chang, 'What is Buddha?' The master replied, 'It seems that the one who sits on the back of the bull is searching for the bull.' Ta-an asked again, 'And what when the disciple has seen the Buddha?' The Master replied, 'As if returning home on the back of the bull.' Ta-an again asked, 'I still cannot quite understand, for how shall I guard it?' Master Bai-chang said, 'Be like the herdsman who guards his bull with a stick so that he takes no fodder from another's meadow.' At that Ta-an understood what the master said and no longer inquired of others. Much later the now Master Chang-ching Ta-an used to tell his monks, 'I used to look after a bull. Whenever he went off the road or ventured into grass, I grabbed him by the nose and dragged him back. Whenever he took fodder from others, however little, I beat him and beat him, and so I carried on with this training for a long time. A poor man is he who is driven around by the words and phrases of others! Now the bull has become shining white and stands always before me. Clearly I see him all day long, and even if I wanted to drive him away, he would not go.'

TO THE PREFACE

At the first stage (Searching for the Bull) it was said, 'Desire for gain and fear of loss flare up like a conflagration, and opinions of right and wrong stand up against each other like spears on a battlefield'. At the sixth stage, the battle is over; gain and loss, too, have vanished into nothing. Great peace now prevails, and the erstwhile enemies have become close friends; they talk together and go for walks into the mountains or along the river. Self and other have become one. There had been many mistakes and many questions, the view of the Buddhas and that of sentient beings, torments and deluded opinions, 'birth and death' and Nirvana, the realm of Buddha and the realm of Mara.

At the various stages we were given many Koans to see into, such as The Original Nature of Truth [Dharmakaya Koans] — Acting from this Truth [Differentiation Koans] — [The Koans] On Truth that is Hard to Approach and Hard to Understand — The Five Ranks of Breaking into the Truth — The Ten Grave Precepts. Day and night we struggled through all these many Koans. Now all is over and done with, and the heart too has become devoid of gain or loss. In this free heart, self absorbs in other and other absorbs in self.

There, 'The stone girl dances to the tune of long life, and the wooden man sings the song of peace'. What the herdsman plays on his flute is a simple folk song, not the artificial trills of the skilled musician. Leisurely he spends his days to his heart's content. Now there is nothing to worry about — great white bull, with whom each of us is fully endowed! The great awakening has taken place and now great peace is everywhere. The herdsman is like a noble guest at the emperor's palace. From the splendour of the castle he looks up into the blue sky, surrounded by nobility of heart and noble courage, himself radiating uplift and aspiration.

Yet in all this he is not bound by honour and wealth. He does not shy away from poverty and lowliness, nor from being despised or slandered; fortune and misfortune in everyday life do not affect him. Here is the great leisure, the great peace, the freedom of the heart. This primordial, spacious freedom is the source from which all men have their being. Any action, direct from this source, whatever it might be, is a Buddha-deed. Master Hakuin once said, 'Coming and going yet ever at home. Singing and dancing are the voice of the Dharma'.

TO POEM 1

The herdsman returns home when the evening mists rise. The boundary has gone between delusion and awakening, between then and now. His flute is not made by a skilled master but is rather the 'flute without a hole' of the Zen truth. The melody played, rhythmic but not studied, merges with the evening mist. This is the time of the 'pairing of light and dark'. Step by step, heaven and earth are one; note for note, source of all things. The tune of the flute is like the melody at the source of all things and is called the 'Samadhi of Play'. Only one who has awakened can hear the boundless joy of this song, but he cannot communicate it. This hidden melody of Zen sounds not only in the flute but pertains in all the deeds of one who has awakened. Examples of this melody are:

A monk asked Master Chao-chou [Joshu], 'Has a dog Buddha -Nature?' The Master said, 'No' [MU]. Another monk asked the Master for instructions; Chao-chou said, 'Have you eaten your rice gruel?' The monk answered, 'Yes, I have'. 'Then go and wash your bowl', the Master instructed him. A monk asked the great Master Ma-tsu [Baso], 'What is Buddha?' Ma-tsu replied, 'Neither heart nor Buddha', but when Master Ta-mei [Daibai] had once asked the same question, Ma-tsu had stated, 'Heart is Buddha'. Master Chao-chou when asked by a monk, 'What is the meaning of the First Patriarch Bodhidharma's coming from the West?', replied, 'The oak tree in the front garden'.

All these replies, each in its own way, sing the hidden melody of Zen, but who can hear it, who understand it? It cannot be chanted with the mouth nor heard with the ear. Parents cannot teach it to their children. Only one who has died and been born again, directly understands.

TO POEM 2

When on the way home the herdsman points towards the dyke ahead, that is, when he now reflects on his earlier delusive thoughts, these have already changed into the landscape of home. In the 'recollected unity of differentiation and equality' the afflicting passions are transformed into wisdom. The sound of the flute is so low it can hardly be heard just on the border of audible and inaudible, between light and dark as the pairing of both. When the herdsman now comes out of the mist, all tunes turn into the song of return. An old poem says, 'Twilight already covers the valleys, and on their way back the wood-cutters sing, We return home, we return home!'.

Bai-ya was renowned for playing the harp, and his friend Chung-tsi-tieh could understand and interpret what he played. When Bai-ya played the high mountain, his friend commented, 'Good! Soaring like Mount Tai-shan'. To his playing running water, Ching-tsi-tieh said, 'Wide and broad like the great river.' Yet, the beauty of Master Bai-ya's songs is still within the field of the senses and of intellectual understanding; who ever really heard the hidden melody of Zen can no longer admire elaborate compositions.

When this secret melody has truly been heard how is it then? Master Ling-yuan Reiun, having awakened on seeing the peach blossoms, wrote, 'For thirty years have I been seeking for the true nature; how many times did spring change into autumn! But the instant I saw the peach blossoms, I doubted no longer.' When Master Hsuan-cha [Sensha] heard this poem, he remarked, 'Good, very good, but the old brother Ling-yuan has not yet penetrated to the very bottom'. Master Yun-men [Ummon] commented on this remark, 'Perfect or not-perfect, penetrated or not penetrated, there is no room for either. Train for another thirty years!' These three masters did hear each other well!

TO POEM 3

'Sitting back to front on the bull' does not match the picture; but 'back to front' might indicate that the rider is completely at-one with the gentled bull, and so points at the unimpeded freedom of the herdsman's actions. The bull walks home by himself; for the herdsman, home now is everywhere. Even doing as he likes can no longer be contrary to his original nature, because all his doing arises from the original home and flows back into it. Now the heart is fulfilled.

On the way home the herdsman wears a straw coat and bamboo hat, indicating that although the great Dharma has been attained, this does not change one's looks! Home is wherever the cool wind blows and the feet walk. The boundary between worldly and other-worldly has vanished. The bull, lacking nothing, does not even glance at the grass. No more needs to be said.

VII — BULL FORGOTTEN — MAN REMAINS

There are not two Dharmas. Provisionally only has the bull been set up, somewhat in the nature of a sign-post. He might also be likened to a snare for catching hares, or to a fishing net. Now the herdsman feels as when the shining gold has been separated out from the ore, or as when the moon appears from behind a cloud bank. The one cool light has been shining brilliantly since the time before the beginning.

POEMS

1

The herdsman had already come home on the back of the bull.

Now the bull is forgotten and the man is at ease.

He may still sleep though the sun is high in mid-heaven.

Whip and rein are now useless, and put away under the eaves.

2

Though the herdsman has brought the bull down from the
    mountain, the stable is empty.

Straw coat and bamboo hat, too, have become useless.

Not bound by anything and at leisure, singing and dancing,

Between heaven and earth he has become his own master.

3

The herdsman has returned home. Now home is everywhere.

When both things and self are wholly forgotten, peace reigns all
    day long.

Believe in the peak 'Entrance to the Deep Secret' —

No man can settle down on this peak.

Picture VII

BULL FORGOTTEN – MAN REMAINS

At the sixth stage the seeking herdsman and the bull he searched for have been brought back into the unity of the 'recollected nature'. At this stage the verification of the Dharma has been attained but not yet forgotten! Though the herdsman may hand himself over to the laws of his nature, it is not yet the true awakening, because in the oneness of man and bull, the bull still remains somewhere in the herdsman's conscious or unconscious. This is a deeply hidden and almost unnoticeable obstacle to the genuine freedom of the herdsman.

Now, at the seventh stage, this oneness is also outstripped and left behind. The 'verification of the Dharma' has been attained and is now forgotten. At that the herdsman enters a region where 'the complete awakening is like not-yet awakened'. There he stands, awakened and independent of everything. Between heaven and earth he is his own master.

Master Lin-chi [Rinzai] once said, 'In the lump of red flesh there is a true man of no status. He always goes in and out through the sense gates. Who has not yet seen him and not yet proved him, look, look!' When this true man of no status has once been seen in oneself, then all things return to oneself. Delusion and awakening, gain and loss, right and wrong, good and bad, are all returned to the original equality. Only now can the herdsman become a joyous individual, blissfully all to himself. The light of the original nature shines through all time and space.

TO THE PREFACE

By 'Dharma' is meant the source or original nature of all that is. The Kegon [Flower Ornament] Sutra says, 'The Dharma King is this One Dharma', and the Lotus Sutra says, 'In the world of the ten thousand things there is only the One Dharma, not two, not three.' In the relative there is the difference between good and bad, right and wrong; but in the primordial there is neither good nor bad, neither right nor wrong, only the One Dharma. In this original nature, the One Dharma, bull and herdsman have become One; the Buddha-Nature shines in this oneness and is the quality of non-differentiation.

Only provisionally, as an analogy, has the bull been spoken of, has been set up as a sign-post that points at our own original nature. Though in the primordial there is no Dharma, here there is talk of One Dharma, and of the bull. This bull might be likened to a noose, or a net — of no more use once the hare or the fish is caught. This is expressed in the words, 'Bull Forgotten, Man Remains'.

The analogy of noose and net is from the book of Chuang-tsu, a Taoist text. Not just the bull, all the Sutras, too, are merely as a finger pointing at the moon. The many Koans are only as a stone with which to knock at the front door of one's own home. To mistake the finger for the moon of truth, or the stone for one's own home, is patently wrong. Only with reference to the

'first step of awakening to the nature of truth' can there be said to
be a difference between noose and hare, or between net and
fish. In the realm of the 'original nature of truth' there are no
such differentiations — this is what Master Lin-chi [Rinzai] calls
'the true man of no status'. And yet there is differentiation in
equality and equality in differentiation.

The saying about the moon and gold is found in volume four
of the Ryogon Sutra [Surangama Sutra]. While we are deluded,
the pure gold of our nature is mixed with dross, and the moon of
our heart is obscured by clouds. However, in keeping with his
great vow and aspiration, the herdsman has forged himself by
means of countless Sutras and Koans, has endured innumerable
hammer blows in ascending, and has constantly thrown himself
onto the anvil of the severe master. Now he has come back to his
original home where there is no cloud and no dross, or rather
cloud and dross are brought back to their original unity with
gold and moon. A Zen saying states, 'The clear wind sweeps the
bright moon; the bright moon sweeps the clear wind.' Now all
the Buddhas and patriarchs must cry for help and beg the
herdsman to spare their lives. 'The one cool light' is the original
nature, and is the 'moon of truth' or 'the original face before
father and mother were born'.This one cool light shines in
solitary splendour through all time and space. Here is the region
of the great freedom with no wisdom to seek and no sentient
beings to save. It is said that when Sakyamuni was born he
pointed with one hand up to the sky and with the other to the
earth and proclaimed, 'Between heaven and earth I alone am the
World-Honoured One'. It is a traditional saying, a legend, but it
does point at that one cool light of the original face.

TO POEM 1

The unencumbered herdsman has returned home on the
unencumbered bull; he has attained to the 'original nature of

truth'. Now the bull, or the 'beginning of awakening', has vanished, and the herdsman, or the 'original nature of truth', alone remains. He sits quietly, not doing anything. In terms of training this shows that with great effort and after long practice the herdsman has come into the primordial equality of afflicting passions and wisdom, of 'birth and death' and Nirvana. There is nothing more to attain, nothing more to let go. All that is has returned into the original nature. Now there is home everywhere. Koans, Sutras and collections of records have all become useless. Above there is no Buddha to seek and no sentient beings to assist below. This is the state of the 'true man of leisure who has nothing further to seek'. A matching poem by Master Ikkyu says, 'While I tried not to forget, I always forgot. Now that I have forgotten, I no longer forget anything.' The second line of this poem says the same as 'Bull forgotten, Herdsman remains'. A saying by Master Myoe also fits here, 'Nowadays I no longer labour for rebirth in one of the favourable realms, but leave all just to breathing in, breathing out.'

The sun is already high in the sky, while the herdsman still sleeps in his own house, unencumbered and free of care. Master Jakushitsu expressed this as, 'Deep in the mountains, sitting in bright day-light at the window of the thatched hut, I heard the wind in the pines and fell fast asleep'. Again Master Ikkyu, 'Joyfully I dwell in the house of the great sky, and when sleepy I put my head on Mount Sumeru as pillow!' What peace here! This has nothing to do with a lazy, care-for-nothing life but is the fruit of long and hard training. Yet not even at this stage can the disciple settle down; he must go still further. 'Whip and rein' are the countless old Koans and Sutras which have now become useless like old paper. However, one who takes this 'uselessness' literally is sure to go to hell straight as an arrow. Just where there is no wisdom to seek and no sentient beings to save, there the disciple must venture forth to seek wisdom and to save sentient beings. So keep and take good care not only of all the Sutras and

Koans, and of all scholarly books —but even of potato peelings!

TO POEM 2

The bull is nowhere to be seen; he has become nothing. Here, there is no longer even a nothing. A pointer to what this might mean is given in Case 63 of 'The Blue Cliff Record', (comments in brackets). 'One day the monks of the east hall and those of the west hall quarrelled about a cat. (Perhaps whether the cat had, or had not, Buddha-Nature; or perhaps what Buddha-Nature is.) Master Nan-chuan [Nansen], notified, arrived at the scene, took hold of the cat, and addressed his monks, 'If one of you can say a word, the cat is saved. If not, I'll kill it. Speak, Speak!' No one could answer. With one stroke Master Nan-chuan cut the cat in two. (Great function of Master Nan-chuan! If necessary he would slice up even Yama, the fierce king of hell.) With this one decisive stroke the root of all evil and all misdeeds has been cut off. When Nan-chuan's disciple, Chao-chou [Joshu] returned to the monastery, Nan-chuan told him what had happened and asked, 'What would you do?' Chao-chou took off his straw sandals, put them on his head and went out. Nan-chuan said, 'Had you been here, I could have saved the cat.'

Is the bull in our picture series the same as Nan-chuan's cat, or not? What does taking hold of the cat mean? What the cutting in two? What is Chao-chou [Joshu] showing? Only when these questions have become crystal clear is it possible to fully affirm Nan-chuan's final words to his disciple Chao-chou. Though not immediately obvious, there is an intimate connection between the above story and the 'though the herdsman brought the bull down from the mountain, he is not seen in the stable.'

'Straw coat and bamboo hat' refer to the tools which the disciple for so long has both needed and used. Now Koans,

Sutras and the like have become useless. Great peace and great leisure pervade his everyday life. When hungry, he eats. When tired, he sleeps. For the rest of his life he uses this one cool light and does not exhaust it. When this light unfolds, it fills the whole world. When it contracts, it cannot lighten up the tiniest nook or cranny. No shadow, no worry clouds the heart of the disciple. He is no longer bound by anything — by neither Buddha nor Mara. Here, too, the stone girl dances and the the iron man sings, indicating the realm of the great freedom and the great function. This utter freedom permits of no rules.

TO POEM 3

The herdsman has returned home. Now home is every-where, in the open fields or up in the mountains. He stands within the Buddha-Nature; things and I, bull and self, now and then, all are forgotten. In such forgetting there is peace and clarity all day long. The bull that roamed about wild in the mountains has been brought down and is now gentled. He has become domesticated and walks freely about in the house.

The way of ascending and the way of descending — who never climbed the summit does not know the landscape of ascending; and who never got used to domesticity knows nothing of the circumstances surrounding descending. The scholar who only chases words and books does not know the nature of ascending, the Zen Buddhist who is content with little awakening, knows nothing of descending. Both one and the other are incomplete. In Zen training, the disciple must first climb the high peak and then dare one further step beyond.

The third poem points at that step beyond. Now that home is everywhere, to the herdsman walking along crowded roads is the same as being alone on a mountain peak. Neither partial to the silence on the summit nor bothered by roaring traffic, 'there is peace all day long.'

Master Tien-tai [Tendai] says in a poem, 'The peak Entrance to the Deep Secret is not for human beings. Outside the heart there is nothing. Far range mountains, blue heaped on blue.' On the merit of this poem Fa-yen [Hogen] acknowledged him as his heir with the words, 'With this poem you inherit my school' (Hui-yuan vol. 12). This peak 'Entrance to the Deep Secret' is the original nature of human beings. 'Believe in this peak' means to believe the original nature, believe heaven and hell, believe now and then, believe everything. Worldly desires and afflicting passions, too, once they have been seen into to their very source, are that peak, the original nature of human beings. One who has arrived there can no longer be considered 'dyed a human', though he lives as a man among men. This is why he can lead and teach others.

However, though the bull may have been forgotten, the herdsman himself still remains, and thus also the need for painstaking further training. Thus no-one may settle down on this peak, not even one who has returned home already and so no longer needs to seek the Buddha and search for the Dharma-Truth.

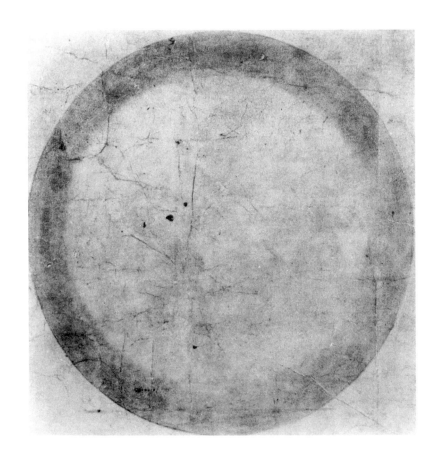

VIII — BOTH BULL AND MAN FORGOTTEN

When all worldly desires have dropped away, holiness, too, has lost its meaning. Do not stay at a place where Buddha is, and quickly pass by where he is not. Not even a thousand eyes can see into the heart of one who clings to neither. Holiness to which birds consecrate flowers is shameful.

POEMS

1

Whip and rein, bull and man, are all gone and vanished.

No words can encompass the blue vault of the sky.

How could snow pile up on a red-hot hearth?

Only when arrived at this place can a man match the old masters.

2

Shame! Up till now I wanted to save the whole world;

Now, what surprise! There is no world to be saved!

Strange! Without ancestors or successors,

Who can inherit, who pass on this truth?

3

Space shattered at one blow and holy and worldly both vanished.

In the Untreadable the path has come to an end.

The bright moon over the temple and the sound of wind in the
tree.

All rivers, returning their waters, flow back again to the sea.

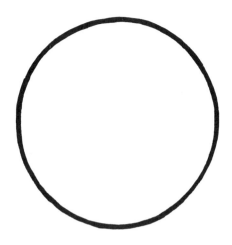

Picture VIII

BOTH BULL AND MAN FORGOTTEN

The hall-mark and pivot of Zen are in the total forgetting of both, man and bull. As referred to in the beginning, 'A special transmission outside the teachings — no dependence on written words — directly pointing to the human heart — seeing into its nature and becoming Buddha'. Zen started with Kasyapa smiling at the Buddha's raising of the flower. It was handed down by twenty-eight Indian patriarchs until it reached Bodhidharma who brought it to China. There it was transmitted further till it came to the Sixth Patriarch Hui Neng [Eno]. In the transmission after Hui-Neng, five branches developed, known as the Yun-men [Ummon], Lin-chi [Rinzai], Tsao-tung [Soto], Kuei-yang [Igyo], and Fa-yen [Hogen] schools. Of these, only the Lin-chi school has an unbroken transmission reaching up to today.

The special nature of Zen lies outside the Buddhist teachings; in and for itself it neither admits nor needs intellect and scholarship. It rather is 'a life apart which is also another life', that is, the complete and utter forgetting of bull and herdsman. Having thus forgotten, the disciple neither venerates the holy masters nor makes much of his own spirit. The heart becomes empty, the situation peaceful, and the body is just as it is.

Once this is attained, the heart-mirror is clear and spacious emptiness opens wide. Arriving there, a man lets go of delusion and does not hold to wisdom. He dwells neither in delusion nor in awakening, is neither worldly nor holy. All worldly desires have dropped off and at the same time the meaning of holiness has become empty. This being detached from everything is what Master Lin-chi [Rinzai] expressed by 'Suddenly snatching away both man and circumstance.' Here the disciple passes through the absolute nothing in which essence and form, self and things, all become NOTHING. True and genuine Zen experience is just the 'snatching away both man and circumstance'.

This utter NOTHING is the source from which all thinking and all knowing arise, but calling it the source is only provisional, relative. No words, not even names such as 'the unborn', Nirvana, or 'absolute truth' can reach there because it is before all words and concepts and even before thinking! Master Te-shan [Tokusan] once said to his monks, 'Whether you can say it or not, either way thirty blows!'

TO THE PREFACE

The disciple first shattered the 'realm of worldly desires and afflicting passions' and at stage seven broke into the 'realm of the holy'. Now at stage eight even the realm of the holy has vanished. Neither worldly nor holy, only now is he capable of inheriting the living wisdom of Buddhas and patriarchs, is he 'above all Buddhas and masters', and has become a man of Zen who has settled the 'one great matter'. This is the crux of Zen training. For here all afflicting passions drop off, and holiness, too, loses its meaning. The place where the Buddha dwells is the world of differentiation, the world of the changing forms. There the herdsman must not stay and settle down. And the place of no Buddha is the realm of equality, of non-differentiation, in which neither essence nor changing forms have any meaning; there the herdsman must quickly pass by. Master Yung-chia [Yoka Daishi] says in his 'Song of the Realization of the True Way', 'Even truth has no meaning there, for the primordial is devoid of delusion. When both being and non-being drop off together, the not-empty voids itself too, and that is called truth.' · There is then nothing relative acknowledged as relative, nothing absolute prized as absolute. The absolute is through the relative, the relative through the absolute. We err in the relative if we acknowledge it as relative , and we err in the absolute if we prize it as absolute. In the utter forgetting of bull and herdsman, the relative as the relative, and the absolute as the absolute, cancel each other out.

The phrase 'neither the one nor the other' refers to all pairs of opposites, such as now and then, Buddha and Mara, equality and differentiation. No way of thinking or saying can lead into the innermost of one who is not attached to either the one or the other. In his record on 'Faith in the Heart' the Third Patriarch says, 'Do not attach to either the one or the other! Do not seek after it! When clinging ever so slightly to right or wrong, the heart gets entangled. Two arise from the one, but do not cling to the one either. Not being attached to anything, delusion cannot arise.'

The saying about the birds reverently bringing flowers comes from the following story: 'Master Niu-tou [Gozu] used to meditate diligently in a stone cave near Yu-chi-shi temple on Mount Niu-tou. Birds reverently brought him flowers, admitting his outstanding virtues. When later Niu-tou had inherited the

Dharma from the Fourth Patriarch Tao-hsin [Doshin], the birds
stopped bringing him flowers.'

A man to whom birds bring flowers is still attached to
holiness; he has not yet attained to the utter forgetting of bull
and herdsman.

TO POEM 1

There is no dust in the primordial. The great sea of wisdom
has no waves. All Sutras and Koans are left behind, and wisdom
and Nirvana have also become useless. This is Master Lin-chi's
'Snatching away man and circumstance'. The boundary has
vanished between Buddha and Mara, now and then. Everywhere is clear and transparent. At the instant self and Koan
become one, there is no longer a self or a Koan, nor a 'become
one', not even a 'there is nothing anymore'! No thinking can
reach there. An old Chinese poem echoes it, 'My husband went
north, crossing Bai-lang-ho river, and of late no letter has come
from him. South of Dan-feng-cheng castle where I await his
return, the autumn evenings are long.'

The utter forgetting of bull and herdsman is the last gate on
the way of ascending. Here the great fires flare in which all
things are burnt away. 'When you meet the Buddha, kill the
Buddha; when you meet the patriarchs, kill the patriarchs.'
Good and bad, right and wrong, wisdom and delusion, all
vanish as completely as snow on a red-hot hearth.

In volume five of the Hui-yuan we are told that Master
Chang-bi [Chomei], after having been to the tomb of the Sixth
Patriarch in the province of Ling-nan, visited Master Shih-tou
[Sekito] who asked him, 'Where do you come from?' 'From
Ling-nan'. 'Did you complete your training there?' 'Long ago,
but the eye is still lacking.' Shih-tou commented, 'Do you need
an eye to put into your forehead?' When Chang-bi asked for
further instruction, Shih-tou, who was sitting with crossed legs,

stretched out one of his legs. Chang-bi bowed respectfully. Shih-tou asked, 'You bow; what have you seen?' Chang-bi said, 'As I see it, it is like snow on a red-hot hearth.'

Only here, at this place which is above all Buddhas and patriarchs, has the herdsman attained to the essence of Zen. It, and the life of it, is precisely this utter forgetting of bull and herdsman.

TO POEM 2

I undertook the laborious task of training myself by means of Sutras and Koans because I wanted to rescue all sentient beings. Looking back now, how wonderful, all that is has been Buddha since the very beginning and even cat and spoon are endowed with the wisdom and virtue of Buddha. I am ashamed at my previous conceited pretensions.

We cannot but shiver at this — thank you! But above all it is a disgrace to let sentient beings become nothing.

In this realm, nothing arises and nothing ceases; there is no birth and no death. Past and future are contained in the here and now, which fills the whole universe. Seen from this here and now, Sakyamuni was not born, Bodhidharma did not come to China. Here spontaneity and immediacy rule supreme. Of this one way of ascending it is said that not even sages or saints can transmit it, and yet, it must be transmitted.

Kasyapa smiled at the Buddha's holding up the flower. Was there a transmitting and inheriting? No. Was there no transmitting nor inheriting? But there was. Thus the transmission of non-transmission. When Ananda asked Kasyapa, 'Beside the robe of gold brocade, was there anything else that Sakyamuni transmitted?', Kasyapa called, 'Ananda!' On Ananda's answering, 'Yes?', Kasyapa told him, 'Push over the flag-pole at the temple gate!' This is an example of the transmission of non-transmission.

TO POEM 3

The shattering of the great sky is the complete forgetting of bull and herdsman. The great sky was shattered, for example, by Bodhidharma's 'vast and empty nothing holy!', by Chao-chou [Joshu] with his 'MU' [No]; by Hakuin with his 'Sound of the Single Hand'; by Bankei with his 'Unborn'; by Yun-men [Ummon] with his almost meaningless expletives like 'Gu!', 'Kan!', or 'E!', and by Lin-chi with his mighty 'Ho!' [Katsu].

'No roof over the head, no ground beneath the feet' is an old Zen saying. In the untreadable the path comes to an end.

Still, the disciple must not stop even where the path comes to an end. In the untreadable a change occurs, and suddenly a new way opens which is actually the old way. Then the bright moon shines in front of the temple and the wind blows. A famous Zen saying states, 'Into the clearest the tips of the grasses; into the clearest the master's heart.' The Buddha-Nature is present even in the tips of grass stalks. Men and women, old and young, pots and pans, cat and spoon, all and everything flow back into the realm of the Buddha, or rather, has already just as it is, become Buddha. Even though this great awakening is already entered into, it is still necessary to continue forging oneself until put into one's coffin — and still further on in lives to come. Even Sakyamuni and Bodhidharma are still training.

The Buddha's wish is for infinite, endless ascending. 'The Dharma-Gates [Dharma teachings or teachings of the truth] are manifold; I vow to learn them all. The Buddha Way is supreme; I vow to tread it to the end.'

IX — RETURN TO THE ORIGIN, BACK TO THE SOURCE

In the origin all is pure and there is no dust. Collected in the peace of 'wu-wei', the wonderful action of non-action where all wilful doing has ceased, he beholds the coming and going of all things. No longer deluded by shifting phantom pictures, he has nothing further to learn. Blue runs the river, green range the mountains; he sits by himself and beholds the change of all things.

POEMS

1

Returned to the origin, back at the source, all is completed.

Nothing is better than suddenly being as blind and deaf.

Inside his hermitage, he does not look out.

Boundless, the river runs as it runs. Red bloom the flowers just
as they bloom.

2

The great activity does not pander to being or not being.

And so, to see and to hear he need not be as one deaf and
blind.

Last night the golden bird flew down into the sea,

Yet today as of old, the red ring of dawn flares up in the sky.

3

Done is what had to be done, and all ways are completed.

Clearest awakening does not differ from being blind and deaf.

The way he once came has ended under his straw sandals.

No bird sings. Red flowers glow in crimson splendour.

Picture IX

RETURN TO THE ORIGIN, BACK TO THE SOURCE

Before awakening, mountains are mountains, and water is water. Training under a wise master, on sudden awakening, mountains are not mountains and rivers are not rivers; willows are not green, flowers are not red. However, if we steadily continue on the way of ascending and arrive at this 'source and origin', the mountain is again wholly a mountain, the river is again a river; the willow is green and the flower is red. 'Complete awakening is like not-yet awakened', in spite of the yawning gulf between the two.

In volume four of the Hui-yuan [Goto Egen], in the chapter on Master Ta-mei [Daibai], it is recounted, 'Followers of the Way, turn round your hearts and return to the source! Do not search for what has arisen from it! When you have attained to the source, what has arisen comes to you of itself. If you want to know the source then look into your own original heart. For this heart is the source of all things, whether worldly or transcendent. Therefore, when the heart moves, all the ten thousand things arise; when the heart empties itself, the ten thousand things are gone, too. When the heart is not driven around by either good or bad, everything is just as it is!

Before the disciple can attain to the great suchness of everything, to the great Yes, he must first traverse absolute nothingness and, indeed, let even that nothingness come to nothing. Just where the greatest experience, absolute nothingness, becomes nothing, there it changes into the Great Yes to all that is. Only here is each and everything unconditionally affirmed, and the real life of Zen emerges in all its vitality.

The eighth stage refers to the essence [non-differentiation], the ninth stage to the ten thousand things [differentiation]. The turnover from the unconditional No to the unconditional Yes is, at the same time, the return-flow of the ten thousand things into the one nature [essence]. Equality is differentiation, differentiation is equality. This is the cyclic flow of the Zen life that knows no let nor hindrance, and is clean from its beginning, without any dust. This Zen life is in each human being and is equally in Buddha and also in all things and is the same in all, none has more, none less.

In the real world, the green mountain is wholly the green mountain, and the blue river wholly the blue river. All conditioned things are but the differing forms of the original nature.

TO THE PREFACE

From the beginning, that is from before the beginning of the world, all beings — monks and lay people, cat and spoon, grass, trees and countries — are already Buddha. A man who has returned to his beginning is called 'a man whose heart is formless'. Here a great Yes is said to the world in its reality. Great peace, great joy, and great freedom prevail.

All that exists is subject to change, is impermanent. While one comes to be and grows, another withers away and ceases to be. In the midst of all this growing and declining of everything there is One who dwells in the collected silence of non-doing. Master Lin-chi once said of him that 'he stands amid the traffic of a busy street and yet never turns away from himself.' Even at his busiest he remains always at home — amid all the circumstances of differentiation he yet always dwells in the undifferentiated nature of equality. 'He acts and at the same time does not act, does not act and yet acts.' Thus his doing is the wonderful action of non-doing, the Buddha deed. The Diamond Sutra says, 'Thus shall you look upon this fleeting world: a star at dawn, a bubble in a stream, a flash of lightning from a summer cloud, a flickering lamp, a phantom and a dream.' However, even in the midst of all this impermanence, the activity that has its source in the original nature cannot be misled by any changing forms of this world. Once arrived there, the gradual training as described in the Bull Pictures is no longer needed. And yet, from birth, we still must forge and temper ourselves until we die.

The layman Su Tung-po [Sotoba] said, 'The murmuring brook in the valley is the voice of truth; the green mountain is the body of purity.' A poem by Han-shan sings, 'The old pine tree, swaying in the wind, murmurs wisdom. The bird, gently chirping, proclaims the truth.' These express the same as 'Blue flows the river, green range the mountains.'

TO POEM 1

After long and hard training, the disciple has come to the origin. There the willows are again green and the flowers are again red, just as they once were. All the ten thousand things arise from the one truth. Now the disciple realizes that his search for the bull was unnecessary labour. Complete awakening is like not-yet-awakened. Legend says that though the fish has already become a dragon, yet its scales have remained the same! Even though a man has attained to the great awakening, his looks remain unchanged. Master Lin-chi said, 'After all there is nothing special in Huang-po's [Obaku] teachings.' Only Lin-chi can express it like this; imitated by somebody not yet arrived at the source, his words would in essence differ from Lin-chi's, and so Lin-chi's saying, without imitation, can be truly affirmed only when returned to the source after long and bitter training.

It is a false Zen to plunge into nothing and to get stuck there where no forms can be seen, no voice can be heard, where there is no Buddha and no Mara. Instead, one is to enter the busy city, there to see yet not to see, not to see yet see. Between heaven and earth, only one ear; between heaven and earth, when seeing and what is seen have both vanished, only one eye.

Inside the hut to see what is outside, or when outside to see what is in the hut, such fancy tricks are not the genuine truth, not the genuine seeing. The poem says, 'He sits in his hut and sees not what is outside.' All things are as they are; here essence turns into form. This is the Middle Way of Suchness.

TO POEM 2

He is no longer constrained either by what he does nor by the doing itself. This spontaneous doing is the 'wonderful doing of non-doing'. When hearing and seeing in utter detachment from seeing and hearing, then everywhere is deliverance. Nor is there any more need to be deaf and blind, for the above hearing and seeing itself is the 'wonderful doing of non-doing'.

Everything is as it always has been. 'Yesterday evening I ate three bowls of rice, this morning five bowls of gruel.' This is the great affirmation of all that is just as it is. Master Lin-chi calls it, 'Snatching away the man but not the circumstance.' 'Yesterday, today, it is as it is. The sun rises in the sky and the moon sets. In front of the window the mountains range far, and deep runs the river.'

TO POEM 3

Searching for the bull, the herdsman has exhausted all the strength of his heart. Now he has come to the end of all ways. He has rediscovered his original, formless, non-doing nature. No longer in need of deliverance from delusion or from the afflicting passions, he has no need to look for wisdom. Even clearest awakening is of no use to him any more, for neither it nor the highest knowledge could have made him attain to this place. Nor does clearest awakening differ from the life of a peasant who 'uses it every day without knowing it'. This not-knowing becomes intimate familiarity.

Yet, clearest awakening is not mere deafness and blindness. Just by virtue of being blind and deaf he must be able to move freely and without hindrance, must have the clearest understanding in all situations. He must be able to lead his disciple freely and according to circumstances, sometimes with thirty blows of the stick, sometimes with a great 'Ho' [Katsu], and sometimes with his tiny tongue. This vitality of the Zen life that wells up from the blindness and deafness should be well heeded. Once arrived at the origin, the way has come to an end. Han-shan said in one of his poems, 'For ten years I have lived on this mountain and have forgotten the way I came'. This saying, like the third line of the poem, points to where the way of ascending leads.

With no bird singing, the mountain is even more still. This is the original and ultimate silence in which there is NOTHING; and yet in this NOTHING is an inexhaustible potential. Out of the original and ultimate silence the red flowers bloom in crimson splendour. The herdsman has returned to his ordinary self and yet lives in the untreadable.

X — ENTERING THE MARKET-PLACE
WITH BLISS-BESTOWING HANDS

The brush-wood gate is firmly shut and neither sage nor Buddha can see him. He has deeply buried his light and permits himself to differ from the well-established ways of the old masters. Carrying a gourd, he enters the market; twirling his staff, he returns home. He frequents wine-shops and fish-stalls to make the drunkards open their eyes and awaken to themselves.

POEMS

1

Bare-chested and bare-footed he enters the market,

Face streaked with dust and head covered with ashes,

But a mighty laugh spreads from cheek to cheek.

Without troubling himself to work miracles, suddenly dead
trees break into bloom.

2

In friendly fashion this fellow comes from a foreign race,

With features like those of a horse, or again like a donkey.

But on shaking his iron staff, all of a sudden

All gates and doors fly wide open for him.

3

From out of his sleeve the iron rod jumps right into the face.

Genially and full of laughter,

He may talk Mongolian, or speak in Chinese.

Wide open the palace gates to him who, meeting himself, yet
remains unknown to himself.

Picture X

ENTERING THE MARKET-PLACE
WITH BLISS-BESTOWING HANDS

Who in himself has let the verification of truth ripen completely, he then goes into the world to assist others. As did all Buddhas and patriarchs, he gives himself into and collects himself in this assisting. Prompted by his deep compassion, he throws himself into the dusty world and by virtue of the great vow he reaches out a helping hand to rescue all beings. Can his action be called moral or religious? No, neither. The vitality of Zen pervades all his doings freely and unhindered and is not confined by moral or religious regulations. No one can define his playful and free-wheeling life. Itself beyond all rules and moral laws, it is yet at the same time the place from which all moral and religious norms arise.

Such a being arises at will from, or again dives into the realm of Buddha, or into Mara's domain, into wisdom or into the afflicting passions. He hides his enlightened nature and may frequent wine-shops and fish-stalls to help the drunkards there to awaken to themselves. This is the self-absorption and re-collection in the play of the original nature.

In the second volumes of the Hui-yuan [Goto Egen] we find the story of Pu-tai [Hotei]. 'The priest Pu-tai was from the province of Feng-hua; his other name was Chi-chi. He was a small man, with low forehead and a big belly. His talk could be very odd, and he just laid himself down whenever sleep overcame him. He wandered about begging, carrying all his belongings, including a shabby meditation cushion, in a large sack dangling from his staff. In March of the third year Chen-ming of the Liang dynasty, Pu-tai was about to die. Sitting on a rock at the Yua-lin-shi temple, he sang, 'Maitreya! True Maitreya! Though inherent in all the countless beings, yet you hide yourself in them! To the people here you always show yourself but nobody recognizes you.'

The above song indicates who Pu-tai was. Maitreya is said to be the next Buddha to appear and save all those who as yet had no affinity link with the Buddha-Dharma or had no opportunity to hear it expounded. Maitreya, it is believed, complements Sakyamuni.

Fundamentally , he represents the proof and verification of the great vow to assist all sentient beings now and in the future. Pu-tai as a manifestation of Maitreya turned away from the well established paths of the old masters so as to save ordinary people in cities and villages. His talk and manner were startling to all.

The yearning of our heart is to clearly see into our original nature. That being fulfilled, we are at once to undertake assisting sentient beings, which entails entering the world of differentia-tion, 'entering the market-place with bliss-bestowing hands.'

TO THE PREFACE

The brush-wood gate is firmly barred. One who has awakened keeps his nature and way covered up and lets neither worldlings nor holy ones enter. Heaven and earth, the way of ascending and the way of descending, have all vanished. He neither looks up to the saints nor esteems his own spirit. Sakyamuni's holding up the flower, Vimalakirti's 'Thundering Silence', Chao-chou's [Joshu] 'Have you drunk your tea?', or the 'Sound of the Single Hand', all point at the place of the barred brush-wood gate. This place is in all masters; nobody can enter it. But the barring of the gate is at the same time an opening of the door and reaching out a hand to help others to enter. The last stage after the way of ascending is also called 'secret of secrets' or 'wonder of wonders'. This region where there is nothing at all is the very source of poetry and of a deep and quiet humanity.

The rest of the Preface is concerned with assisting others. He mixes with saints and worldlings, Buddhas and Mara, with the just and the unjust, with good and bad arising here and vanishing there, or vice versa. All the masters up till now, once they had arrived at their completion, gave themselves to the work of rescuing others. However, from of old the ways of carrying out this task were highly individual. They might sometimes go along well established ways, or take very different routes; there are no rules for it. Pu-tai's way was most unusual. He hid his enlightened being in the form of a beggar-monk, intentionally turned away from the rules hallowed of old and generally behaved strangely, appearing and disappearing in towns and villages. In the Zen school, there always were such individual paths — Manjusri, Vimalakirti, Pu-tai, Han-shan, Shi-te, etc. Pu-tai's way originates and flows from his heart and so trying to imitate him would be nonsense.

The sentence 'Now he enters . . . now he returns . . .' points at the spontaneity of his actions, his free and unhindered doing which is rooted in his great compassion. According to an old Zen saying, 'Long ago when I went away, I walked through flowering meadows. Now I am returning home through the falling leaves.' He immerses himself and collects himself in the play of saving others. 'On the road he is not away from home; away from home he is not on the road' (Lin-chi). 'Seeing form, he is not deluded by form; hearing sounds, he is not deluded by sound' (Lin-chi). This kind of being is called 'Lotus in the Fire' or 'Jewel in the Mud '. Master Lin-chi expounded on this free play of rescuing others:

'This man is not obstructed by anything. He penetrates the whole universe and moves about in the three worlds without let or hindrance. In the world of forms he is not obstructed by forms. In an instant he enters the world of truth. When he meets the Buddha, he teaches the Buddha; when he meets an Arhat, he teaches the Arhat; when he meets a Hungry Ghost, he teaches the Hungry Ghost. Roaming about at will, everywhere he assists those lost in the world, yet never runs away from the One. The pure light penetrates the whole universe, and in its light all things are one. Followers of the Way, the courageous man knows right now that in the origin there is nothing.'

The afflicting passions are themselves the Buddha-Nature, and all things without exception are Buddha. 'Helping all sentient and inanimate beings to become Buddha', the source of this vow, as well as of the other three, is just the place of the firmly barred brush-wood gate. The Four Great Vows (see below) are the foundation of the Zen Way and the heart of all Buddhas and patriarchs.

TO POEM 1

With an open, giving heart he merges with light and with dust. How can such a one be called? An independent, open-hearted, true man? A fool? Or a holy one? He is a 'holy fool'.

He hides nothing. Once Master Hui-tang accompanied by the layman Huang Shan-gu went for a walk. Suddenly a wonderful scent of flowers surrounded them. Hui-tang asked, 'Do you smell the flowering mignonettes?' On Huang Shan-gu's 'yes', Hui-tang said, 'I am not hiding anything from you.' At that, Huang Shan-gu suddenly awakened.

'His face streaked with dust, the head covered in ashes', like a fool he wanders around all day in the town, that is in the world of dust. Willingly he dives into the painfully heaving sea of birth and death to save those drowning in it. Without building temples he has the dignity of a Buddha. Whatever he playfully lays his hands on becomes truth and shines in primordial light. Nobody can see into or find out about this play. A great laugh spreads over his face.

'Miracles' in the last lines refer to magic and miracles. However, in the true Dharma there is no magic, neither secrets nor miracles; who believes in them treads an erroneous path. True, in Zen there are all kinds of ingenious devices such as to let Mount Fuji emerge from out of a tea kettle, or to squeeze water from a red-hot pair of fire tongs; or to sit down inside a wooden post, or else to let two mountains change place with each other. However, that is not magic and nothing wonderful or strange, just ordinary triviality.

'. . . the dead trees suddenly break into bloom'. We remember the vow, 'Sentient beings are numberless, I vow to assist them all'. He lets ordinary, worldly people suddenly, here and now, become Buddha. In terms of the training, this means leaping out of the great No into the great Yes.

The 'holy fool' is the inexhaustible creative play of primordial life. Here original being is itself at play — though there is no such thing as original being!

TO POEM 2

'This fellow' is the priest Pu-tai [Hotei]. He comes from a foreign race — he does not necessarily observe the religious rules. Being neither worldly nor holy, he is neither compelled by afflicting passions nor does he dwell in wisdom. In a friendly way he comes to us from this wondrous region, from the region of no-thing-ness, of non-differentiation, into the world of the manifold differentiations. Entering it, after having passed through NO-THING, this one world of differentiation is itself a world of unlimited freedom and inexhaustible creativity. Now he lives in it 'without light and yet full of light'.

The second pair of lines of the poem concern this illimitable freedom and unimpeded spontaneity of action. He enters one house with the face of a horse, and another showing the features of a donkey. Now he appears to be a worldling, then again a Buddha — a holy one, a fool, a donkey.

With one stroke of his staff he shatters everything and a spacious roomy emptiness opens. Door and gate, the realm of Buddha and that of Mara, Nirvana and Birth-and-Death shatter and everything becomes transparently clear. 'The cool wind sweeps the bright moon. The bright moon sweeps the cool wind.' This cool, clear, wind blows through the gentle labour of assisting others.

TO POEM 3

Each word he utters is like an iron rod that jumps out of his sleeve straight into the disciple's face. Each blow is a hit that infallibly cuts through all knots.

However, 'straight into . . . face' may also be understood in the sense that if somebody with a stick should try to hit his face, Pu-tai could easily parry with skilful words (Mongolian or Chinese) and end the quarrel with a great laugh! This latter interpretation seems to be the more likely one. The reader may choose for himself.

'He may speak Mongolian or in Chinese' also means that sometimes he says 'non-existent' and sometimes 'existent', sometimes he teaches 'Heart is Buddha', sometimes 'Neither Heart nor Buddha'. Yet what he says is always quite clear and unmistakable. 'Genially and full of laughter' points at something inexpressible and beyond description.

The next couple of lines raise Master Lin-chi's 'To meet him yet not know him, to talk with him yet not know his name.' The 'self' referred to in the poem is neither man nor woman, neither monk nor layman. When the disciple or lay person knows how to meet this self and yet not to know it, he becomes one with it in intimate familiarity. This is the time of 'Nothing further to do'. If the disciple or layman enters this region of nothing further to do, the palace gates open wide. He has come back home.

Postscript

The essence of Zen is found neither in science, nor in philosophy, nor in the Buddhist teachings, not even in Zazen, which is Zen. It is just a matter of seeing into the Buddha-Nature that is inherent in all sentient beings.

For a really courageous man it is possible to become Buddha in an instant. A lazy one will never even get near Nirvana. With full determination we can and must suddenly jump into the realm of the Buddha. Yet even there we must not stop but rather by virtue of the Great Vows and the Great Compassion we must enter the world of differentiation, our world as we know it, and there immerse ourselves in rescuing others.

So the natural task of all the Buddhas and patriarchs, and of all the masters up till now, is also ours and is expressed in the Four Great Vows, 'Sentient beings are numberless, I vow to assist them all. The afflicting passions are innumerable, I vow to eradicate them all. The Dharma-Gates [teachings] are manifold, I vow to learn them all. The Buddha Way is supreme, I vow to tread it to the end.'

These Four Great Vows may be summarized as 'To look for wisdom above, and to rescue sentient beings below.' Thus the vocation of a Zen Buddhist is to strive ever on and up, spurred by the aspiration of these vows.

I would like to end my comments with this old poem by the Chinese Zen poet Su Tung-po [Sotoba]:

Rain and mist on Mount Ro, and waves surging in Setsu
    river.
My longing to see them would not be stilled.
So I went and came back — just as it is, nothing special —
Rain and mist on Mount Ro, waves surging in Setsu river.

Epilogue by Hartmut Buchner

(Abridged)

The text of the 'Ten Bull Pictures' is still used for training purposes in Japan.

Master Daizokutsu Rekido Otsu, master of the Zen monastery Shokoku-ji in Kyoto, Japan, himself near retirement, kindly permitted publication of his comments to the text. Such publication of a Zen master's Teisho comments is extremely rare and precious even in Japan, as traditional masters do not normally allow their insight and wisdom to be written down and made available to a wider circle; they directly address students in training under them.

This book was compiled from a series of such Teisho talks on the 'Ten Bull Pictures' which Master Otsu gave in 1957 to his monks and lay students. With his permission these were taken down for the purpose of publication in German.

In his general Introduction, Master Otsu says that the pictures are by Master Kuo-an (about 1155). This may offend the historic sense of the Westerner, for Kuo-an's Bull Pictures are lost. Yet they served many generations of painters as models in their own portrayals of the bull. It is entirely in keeping with the Japanese sense of reverence for tradition to consider all these faithful copies as also by Master Kuo-an.

The pictures actually reproduced here are by the Zen painter Shubun (died 1454), who was a monk in the Shokoku-ji monastery and the paintings are still kept there. They are considered today as the most beautiful and also the most exact copies of Kuo-an's pictures. Shubun himself was the teacher of Sesshu (1420-1505) whose work is widely appreciated even in the West.

Special and respectful thanks are due first of all to Zen Master Daizokutso Rekido Otsu for his comments, for the calligraphy he wrote for this edition, and for permission to reproduce the pictures. Thanks also go to the members of the Zen lay community Chishokai who taped and transcribed the Teisho comments, and to Master Otsu's disciple Master Dr. Sonin Kaziya (Kyoto) for the editing and final preparation of the Japanese MS. However the most sincere thanks are due to Professor Dr. Koichi Tsujimura, professor of philosophy of Kyoto University and himself a student of Zen. It was he who first suggested publication, and without his ever ready, loyal and untiring assistance during the period of his stay in Germany, it could not have taken shape. With Master Otsu's permission, he has abridged some very few passages which would have been meaningless to a German reader. Also, some of the frequent repetitions have been omitted without, however, detracting from the traditional style in which such Teisho comments are delivered.

München-Pasing, October 1957   *Hartmut Buchner*

Master Otsu specially brushed these two characters for the book.

Nothing Holy!

The first 'Case' of the Blue Cliff Record concerns the story of Bodhidharma's meeting with emperor Wu-ti of the Liang Dynasty. From it, the relevant passage is as follows:

> The emperor asked the Great Master, 'What is the essence of Buddhism?'
>
> Bodhidharma replied, 'Vast emptiness, nothing holy!'
>
> The emperor asked again, 'Who then is the one who stands before Us?'
>
> Bodhidharma answered, 'Not known.'

Picture VIII of the Bull-Series is comparable to both of Bodhidharma's replies.